TOWARD A PERFECT LOVE
THE SPIRITUAL COUNSEL OF WALTER HILTON

Walter Hilton

Translated and Introduced by

Dr. David L. Jeffrey

MULTNOMAH · PRESS

Portland, Oregon 97266

Other *Classics of Faith and Devotion:*
  Real Christianity by William Wilberforce
  The Reformed Pastor by Richard Baxter
  Sin & Temptation by John Owen
  The Love of God by Bernard of Clairvaux
  A Life of Prayer by St. Teresa of Avila
  The Benefit of Christ by Juan de Valdés and Don Benedetto
  Religious Affections by Jonathan Edwards

TOWARD A PERFECT LOVE
This translation
© 1985 by Multnomah Press
Portland, Oregon 97266

Printed in the United States of America

Library of Congress Cataloging-in-Publication Data

Hilton, Walter, d. 1396.
  Toward a perfect love.

  (Classics of faith and devotion)
  Bibliography: p.
  Includes index.
  Contents: Letters to a layman—Coming to perfection.
  1. Spiritual life—Catholic authors.   I. Jeffrey, David L., 1941-   .
II. Hilton, Walter, d. 1396. Scale of perfection. 1985.   III. Title.   IV.
Series.
BX2349.H54   1985   248.4'82   85-15470
ISBN 0-88070-103-X

85 86 87 88 89 90 – 10 9 8 7 6 5 4 3 2 1

CONTENTS

Preface to the Classics   ix

Translator's Preface   xiii

Introduction   xvii

LETTERS TO A LAYMAN

I. To One New in Faith   3
II. On the Mixed Life   7
Notes

COMING TO PERFECTION *

I. Book One: The Spiritual Life

Salutation   39

Chapter One   41
     TRUE SPIRITUALITY
     The Goal of Contemplation; An Acceptable
     Sacrifice (I: 1; 11- 15)

Chapter Two   47
     ON PRAYER
     The Spirit of Prayer; Types of Prayer (common
     prayer; personal prayer; silent prayer); Effectual
     Prayer (23-33)

---

* parenthetical numbers refer to chapter divisions in the Underhill
transcription

Chapter Three   57
     ON MEDITATION
     The Good of Meditation; The Gift of Meditation
     (34-36)

Chapter Four   61
     EXAMINATION OF CONSCIENCE
     Recognizing our Condition; The Psychology of
     Sin; Health: Our Salvation in Jesus (41-45)

Chapter Five   71
     REFORMATION AND CONTEMPLATION
     Seeking the Lost; The Value of Desire; Where
     and How to Look; Self-Discovery and the Image
     of God (46-55)

Chapter Six   85
     THE MEASURE OF LOVE
     Charity and Appearances; Charity and Judg-
     ment; Truth in the Inward Parts; The Standard
     of Love; Conforming to the Image of Jesus (66-70;
     92-93)

II. Book Two: The Progress of the Soul

Chapter One   99
     THE IMAGE OF GOD
     The Soul As Image; Restoration of the Image
     (II: 1; 4; 5)

Chapter Two   105
     THE SPIRITUAL PILGRIM
     The Road to Jerusalem (21)

Chapter Three   111
     TRUE AND FALSE LIGHT
     Trusting God in the Darkness; Counterfeit Light
     (the Noonday Demon) (25-26)

Chapter Four   119
     LOOKING AT THE SELF
     Spiritual Self-Understanding; Growth in Love;
     Discerning Love's Proper Object; The Reforma-
     tion of Experience; Spiritual Insight; Things
     Seen and Unseen (30-33)

Chapter Five   137

    THE GIFT OF LOVE
    The Source of Love; The Experience of Love;
    The Preeminence of Love; Love and Meekness;
    The Quiet Work of Love (34-40)

Chapter Six   159

    BEHOLDING JESUS
    Beholding Him in Prayer; Jesus in His Word; The
    Still Small Voice; Lord of the Universe; Jesus Our
    Beloved (42-46)

Notes   178

PREFACE TO THE CLASSICS OF FAITH AND DEVOTION

With the profusion of books now being published, most Christian readers require some guidance for a basic collection of spiritual works that will remain life-long companions. This new series of Christian classics of devotion is being edited to provide just such a basic library for the home. Those selected may not all be commonly known today, but each has a central concern of relevance for the contemporary Christian.

Another goal for this collection of books is a reawakening. It is a reawakening to the spiritual thoughts and meditations of the forgotten centuries. Many Christians today have no sense of the past. If the Reformation is important to them, they jump from the apostolic Church to the sixteenth century, forgetting some fourteen centuries of the work of the Holy Spirit among many devoted to Christ. These classics will remove that gap and enrich their readers by the faith and devotion of God's saints through all history.

And so we turn to the books, and to their purpose. Some books have changed the lives of their readers. Notice how Athanasius's *Life of Antony* affected Augustine or William Law's *A Serious Call to a Devout and Holy Life* influenced John Wesley. Others, such as Augustine's *Confessions* or Thomas à Kempis's *Imitation of Christ*, have remained perennial sources of inspiration throughout the ages. We sincerely hope those selected in this series will have a like effect on our readers.

Each one of the classics chosen for this series is deeply significant to a contemporary Christian leader. In some cases, the thoughts and reflections of the classic writer are mirrored in the leader's genuine ambitions and desires today, an unusual pairing of hearts and minds across the centuries. And thus these individuals have been asked to write the introduction on the book that has been so meaningful to his or her own life.

PURPOSE FOR THE CLASSICS: SPIRITUAL READING

Since our sensate and impatient culture makes spiritual reading strange and difficult for us, the reader should be cautioned to read these books slowly, meditatively, and reflectively. One cannot rush through them like a detective story. In place of novelty, they focus on remembrance, reminding us of values that remain of eternal consequence. We may enjoy many new things, but values are as old as God's creation.

The goal for the reader of these books is not to seek information. Instead, these volumes teach one about living wisely. That takes obedience, submission of will, change of heart, and a tender, docile spirit. When John the Baptist saw Jesus, he reacted, "He must increase, and I must decrease." Likewise, spiritual reading decreases our natural instincts, to allow His love to increase within us.

Nor are these books "how-to" kits or texts. They take us as we are—that is, as persons, and not as functionaries. They guide us to "be" authentic, and not necessarily to help us to promote more professional activities. Such books require us to make time for their slow digestion, space to let their thoughts enter into our hearts, and discipline to let new insights "stick" and become part of our Christian character.

James M. Houston

Dr. James M. Houston was born to missionary parents who served in Spain. Dr. Houston served as University Lecturer at Oxford University, England, from 1949-1971. He was a Fellow of Hertford College during the period between 1964-1971, and held the office of Principal of Regent College from 1969-1978. From 1978 to the present he has served as Chancellor of Regent College. He is also Professor of Spiritual Theology for the College.

Dr. Houston has been active in the establishment and encouragement of lay training centers across the continents. These include the C. S. Lewis Institute in Washington, D.C., and The London Institute for the Study of Contemporary Christianity. In addition to his work with the Classics series, he has published a book entitled, I Believe in the Creator (Eerdmans, 1978).

TRANSLATOR'S PREFACE

The editor and translator of Walter Hilton is confronted by an unusually challenging array of obstacles. Although Hilton was English and (somewhat unusually for his time) composed not in Latin but in his native tongue, the qualities of fourteenth-century north-country English and the peculiarities of Hilton's own style are such that translation is far from a straightforward task. No existing text of his work is perfect, and no one modern edition will suffice as an adequate guide.

For the work *Coming to Perfection*, I have translated from the transcription of MS. B. M. Harley 6579 by Evelyn Underhill, and checked against other sources.[1] This treatise is usually titled *The Ladder of Perfection* or *The Scale of Perfection* in early texts. For the work called here *Letters to a Layman*, I have used the MS. transcription by Horstmann of Bodleian MS. Vernon.[2] This work was originally entitled *Epistle on the Medled Life* or *Epistle on the Mixed Life*.

My principles in translation have been simple. I have tried as much as possible to render Hilton in plain, sensible, contemporary English, without sacrificing too much of his own perambulating style in the effort. Hilton has never been thought of as the greatest of stylists, even among the mystics.[3] His flair for eloquent plain talk is considerable but not constant; after thrusts of articulate prose sharp with the truth they carry comes too often a clatter of loose, blunt instruments. No translation can entirely redeem that without deceit. Moreover, one of his most attractive stylistic attributes—his gift for practical example—descends too often, perhaps, to a scrambling of metaphors. And he does tend to repeat himself.

In dealing with these things—frailties for which I fear I am obliged to exercise an empathetic tolerance—I established the following guidelines. In respect of a desire to contain repetition, I have excised some whole chapters from *Coming to Perfection*. Because *Letters to a Layman* is presented in this volume as well, and makes some of the same points, my recension permits altogether a reduction of the text of the larger work by more than a third. Because of my desire to preserve textual integrity, I have translated all the rest of the material as it stands, with the exception of a small deletion from Book II, chapter 5 of *Coming to Perfection*.

This major work was addressed to a woman, but typically and because the information is generalized, Hilton refers to the indifferent third person most often, and only rarely says "she," "her," or "any man or woman." He does, however, refer to the human soul as "it" in situations where we would use a masculine or feminine pronoun or both. I have tried to preserve as much of this neutral language as a reasonable balance of style would permit, but sometimes have amended to the first person plural "we" and "us," or reverted to the third person "one" when that seemed appropriate. These changes also have the effect—a mixed blessing—of making Hilton sound a little less formal to contemporary ears.

Hilton quotes Scripture passages from the available Latin Vulgate text, but evidently always from memory, giving them his own English translations. My practice has been, except in those instances which required that I too use the Vulgate to make sense of his point, to use our own cultural standard, the King James Version. For the most part this works quite faithfully; occasionally I have retained Hilton's English paraphrase as well, when it gives extra strength to the reading.

Numerous good English words used by Hilton no longer, alas, contain the range of meaning once available to them. *Soothfastness*, for example, now requires, depending on the context, to be rendered as *truth, truthfulness,* or *integrity*. The simple word *feeling,* which Hilton employs extensively in *Coming to Perfection,* can mean *touch, experience, spiritual consciousness,* or *perception,* according to context, and I have had to resort to all of these at one point or another to make his meaning clear. In other cases the medieval word simply had more spiritual or psychological weight than does our own equivalent. When Hilton says that an experience is "gracious," he means literally that it is "grace-filled"; when he says that we ought to resist the temptation to "melancholy," he means by that self-pity. And something is lost—though unavoidably—when "highing of thyselfe" has to be rendered as "self-promotion" to ensure a correct understanding. This sort of thing, as well as problems of syntax and punctuation, I have met as well as I knew how. The text which results will, I hope, be readable and enjoyable, without a complete loss of Hilton's own medieval English style and simple country character.

I owe several debts of gratitude: first to Jim Houston, long an admirer of Walter Hilton's writing, who asked me to prepare a translation for this series, and whose own spiritual intuition—and tuition—have been of great value to me. My wife Katherine typed, corrected, queried points of translation, and in general upheld my efforts with her constant and prayerful partnership during these months. My pastor, Patrick Playfair, with his spiritual counsel so like unto Hilton's in its collation of meekness and love, has translated for me "soothfastly" and clearly the simplicity of Jesus' invitation to a burdened soul, helping me to understand at last, as Hilton also says, that all health is in Him—thereby, unknown to himself, richly blessing both translation and translator. Finally, the friend in God, Laird Hamilton, to whom this work is specially dedicated, has been an enduring example to me of a layman whose life is richly grounded in meekness, truth, and love. It is my prayer that readers of this book of Walter Hilton's writings will find in it such an example, and be encouraged to seek a life and vision focused ever more steadfastly upon Jesus.

David L. Jeffrey

---

[1] Walter Hilton, *The Scale of Perfection*, edited from the MSS. by Evelyn Underhill (London: John Watkins, 1923). Professor Underhill corrected by use of several other manuscripts, notably B. M. Harley 2387. I have referred also to a copy of Book I in the Vernon MS. and Trinity College Cambridge MS. 354.

[2] The text begins at fol. 353 in the MS. It is printed by Horstmann in *Yorkshire Writers: Richard Rolle of Hampole and His Followers* (London: Swan, Sonnenschein, 1895-96), vol. I, pp. 264-292.

[3] Dame Julian of Norwich's *Revelations* and *The Cloud of Unknowing* have many passages of great beauty by contrast. But they were never widely known in their own time. Hilton was continuously read by religious and layfolk alike.

INTRODUCTION

Walter Hilton was born some time in the third decade of the fourteenth century, probably in Yorkshire. He spent his last years as an Augustinian canon, living at the nearby Priory of Thurgarton in the county of Nottingham, where he died on March 24, 1396. This makes of him an almost exact contemporary of the great promoter of biblical translation, John Wycliffe.

But more than just a few country miles separate the famous reformer (born also in Yorkshire and nourished by many of the same spiritual sources) from his less politically visible fellow-Christian. Wycliffe from the first was an Oxford academic; he became a controversial philosopher-theologian and also entered vigorously into religious and civil politics by his preaching and by party allegiances. Hilton, by contrast, seems to have begun his life inconspicuously as a layman, then spent some years as a relative recluse following his conversion, until in later years he was to find himself called into a quiet stewardship of souls with the Augustinians. His ministry was never directed to institutions or to the public at large, but to a few individuals, only two of whom are now even known to us. There is no evidence that he ever held an administrative post or position of leadership. No portrait of him exists, visual or verbal. His life is completely unknown to us, except at the point where it emerges to teach and help others. He was, as Evelyn Underhill so eloquently puts it, "one of those hidden figures, those quiet and secret friends of God who have never failed the Church."[1]

The Priory of Thurgarton has largely remained hidden as well. Its ruins, skeletal fragments of window arches and a crumbling tower, are nestled into the soft slope of a hill that rises up gently from what then would have been a very small village. The remains are now a kind of park; not far from the high altar stone of the great church where Hilton would have worshiped, broken pieces of church sculpture form a rock garden. Today's church preserves part of the old Norman nave. In its patina of antiquity the setting is beautiful and tranquil, mirroring, we might think, the tranquillity and composure of Walter Hilton's spiritual writing.

What the modern visitor may not grasp in all this, of course, are the stark realities of Hilton's own fourteenth-century world, realities not less demanding than those of our own time. Six hundred years ago, the most oppressive factors in life, beyond turbulent and explosive political strife, were things that by comparison scarcely trouble us—severe weather and bad health.

Buildings seldom had effective windows; for practical purposes, heating in winter was available only in smokey kitchens and in the great halls of expensive houses, almost never in bedrooms or libraries. There was no equivalent to modern plumbing, and sanitation was, by our standards, wretched. There were no dentists, few physicians, no anesthetics or convenient painkillers, and no known cure for the majority of serious illnesses. Chronic ailments were common and often debilitating; infant mortality was high and life expectancy low. Only a narrow range of foodstuffs would be available in winter, and there was no refrigeration in summer. All of these conditions contribute to homely examples and metaphors in Hilton's writing, but not to complaint.

What he never mentions is his own discomfort or deprivation in his community. Nor do we hear him complain about what then would have been the very serious misery of inclement weather. He does not even speak of bubonic plague, which struck often during his lifetime, and in one epidemic alone, the notorious Black Death of 1348-9, killed as many as half of all people living over most of England. Nevertheless, if he sometimes speaks as though physical life were inferior to our life in heaven, the reader may imagine that Hilton feels the quality of the difference more keenly than most of us are likely to feel it. For all that, his spirituality is, like that of St. Augustine, far less ascetic than the extremes modeled by the desert fathers. Typically for his tradition, he is gentle, balanced, and completely unconcerned to speak about himself or his own spiritual experience.

The Augustinian tradition in Western Christianity has been central to the transmission of biblical values and a Christ-centered spirituality. Augustine's own biblical commentaries and spiritual writings are the most quoted all through the heritage of Christian tradition in the West. But in addition to this general influence there grew up special communities of people who felt called by God to full life-service and who organized their community and spiritual life around a guideline known as the Augustinian Rule. Many great Christian spiritual writers were Augustinians. They include Richard and Hugh of St. Victor, Thomas à Kempis (author of the *Imitation of Christ*), Jan van Ruysbroeck, and of course Martin Luther. Their rule governed the life both of the Augustinian friars, who in the later Middle Ages were often itinerant preachers, and especially the Augustinian canons, of which Hilton was one.

Canons were involved in the ordinary day-to-day workings of the community. Hilton would have had every reason to be familiar with the market life of his village, labor in the fields, and the ordinary necessities of rural and small-town life. His own duties—pastoral work, personal theological study, and teaching—were the chief forms of spiritual service to which the Augustinian canons were called.

Although he was never the pastor of a local church, all of his known writings are pastoral in character. The content of these epistolary treatises is firm, biblically grounded, and uncompromised in its concern to conquer sin. But the tone is wise and kindly, gentle as a shepherd's voice. Hilton sees into ordinary human nature with an almost uncanny perceptiveness, showing us how futile are the disguises with which we mask our weakness, immaturity, self-pity, self-deception, and outright self-centeredness.

Augustinians did not normally train in the manner of seminarians for specific parish duties. Hilton's own theological study in the priory would have been directed first to personal spiritual growth, then to fitting him to give spiritual counsel as that might be required. His writing makes evident that he concentrated his efforts on the Scriptures first, and added to them some of the great spiritual writers of the past, and finally others of his own day. He knew

St. Augustine, St. Gregory, St. Bernard, and St. Bonaventure, and was deeply influenced also by his fellow Yorkshireman Richard Rolle and that other great contemporary spiritual writer, the unknown author of *The Cloud of Unknowing*. He may possibly have been a student for a time at Cambridge, where William Fleet, later spiritual director to Catherine of Sienna, was lecturing; it seems evident that Hilton knew Fleet's books *The Amendment of Life* and *Remedy for Temptations*. If so, his student years did nothing to diminish the rough Yorkshire syntax and rural idiom in which his own work abounds.

Almost every page of Hilton's writings responds to the Bible itself, as he quotes, amplifies, and develops his favorite texts. He seems to have been ahead of Wycliffe in urging laypeople to read the Scriptures in English; he offers the suggestion directly in *Letters to a Layman*, written probably about 1370.[2] Though he certainly wrote some of his work in Latin, he was among the first spiritual writers in the changing culture of fourteenth-century England to write major works in his native tongue, and in them to translate each verse of the Bible following his citation of the Latin text.

Hilton is especially fond of the Gospel of John, the Psalms, the Epistles of Paul, Hebrews, and the Letters of John. Indeed, the reader who wishes a sense of Hilton's spiritual "center" would do well to re-read the fourth Gospel. Afterward, as a preparation for the writings in this book, it would be most helpful to re-read Ephesians 4, 1 John 4, and Hebrews 6; it is almost fair to say that *Coming to Perfection* cannot be fully grasped without these chapters being first in mind.

LETTERS TO A LAYMAN

While he was still living a solitary life, Hilton had written a previous epistolary treatise entitled the *Epistola Aurea* to encourage one Adam Horsley to enter upon a spiritual vocation. We know that Horsley was Chancellor of the Exchequer until 1375, at which point he did indeed leave his post for a spiritual life.[3] These facts, and others, suggest that Hilton did not become a canon at Thurgarton until after 1375. By this reckoning, *Letters to a Layman* (1370) would also have been written while he was still solitary, and much closer himself to his own life as a layman. It is evident, nonetheless, that he was already gifted in the art of spiritual counsel.

The layman to whom this work is addressed remains unknown to us. Evidently he was also a "great lord"—a man of affairs with considerable importance in the commercial or political life of the community. Recently he had had a vital experience of God's Holy Spirit and wanted to follow through on his new commitment as completely as possible. We sense that the man's enthusiasm is real, but perhaps extravagant. He imagines that his new and profound experience of faith will lead him to abandon all of his responsibilities of family, business, and friends to enter into a monastery or religious community as a contemplative. Hilton's first letter has, accordingly, to direct him to consider first the practical opportunities for service in the community and for bodily exercise of his faith. The second letter has two purposes: to encourage him to believe that a profound indwelling of God's Spirit does not automatically entail movement toward what we sometimes think of as "full-time" service, and to believe further that a life in the world can also be a vital spiritual vocation.

As Hilton goes on to develop his theme in the second letter, he attempts to show the layman something of the sanctification of ordinary life. We do not have to leave the world, he says, to experience a rich spiritual growth; indeed, God may be specifically calling us to be *in* the world, though not *of* it, because the world needs to be salted by people who fully accept their temporal responsibilities as undivided from the spiritual service each of us owes to the Lord. Care of the Body of Christ requires that some of his members be such servants.

But Hilton also takes pains to discuss the variety of options open to Christian commitment, and to underscore the values which he believes ought to pertain in each case. The three kinds of life which he identifies are (1) the "active life," by which he means the life of ordinary Christians, who have a modest experience of faith and are preoccupied with life in the secular world; (2) the "contemplative life," by which he means a life much more exclusively dedicated to spiritual service, as in the case of monks or cloistered nuns whose lives are entirely devoted to prayer; and (3) the "mixed life," or middle way, which is the life he is advocating to his correspondent.

The biblical figures which offer themselves to the medieval imagination as types of the first two options are Mary and Martha. Martha, in her diligence to serve practical needs, as well as her preoccupation with these things, was seen as a type of the "active" life. Mary, who sits at the feet of Jesus, oblivious to all the cares of the world, was seen as a type of the "contemplative" life.

What Hilton recommends for this dedicated Christian layman, however, is the "mixed" life, one which learns to make time in the whirl of everyday practical affairs for a true spiritual inwardness, and which develops the resources and potential of spiritual consciousness in a disciplined determination to really look at Jesus, to "contemplate" him. It is in developing a real desire for Jesus, he writes, that any vocation we have is rendered worthy service; all efforts in the world, whether for spiritual service or practical work, are empty unless fully subsumed in our love for him.

COMING TO PERFECTION

This long book-letter was written in two parts. The first of these would seem to have been written in the early 1380s, the second many years later, perhaps just before Hilton's death in 1396. They were both written for the same woman, an anchoress, or enclosed nun, the first as an encouragement to her coming to terms with inner spiritual life, the second to further growth. Although these works had thus an exclusive audience, "Book I" was clearly passed on to others. It rapidly gained such popularity that we have twenty-five early manuscripts still remaining. We have, also, fifteen manuscripts of "Book II." Both were also copied in manuscript together, and at the end of the fifteenth century the *Ladder of Perfection*, as it was then called, was one of the first spiritual books to be printed in England, appearing under the mark of Wynkyn de Worde's Press in 1494.[4] Demand for it grew steadily, and its influence was such that for some time the authorship of the *Imitation of Christ* was also ascribed to Hilton. It remains in fact the most widely influential of all English medieval spiritual books.

The original title has its roots in the story of Jacob's ladder, and like the children's hymn, it visualizes spiritual growth in the Christian life as a movement from earth to heaven, from the slavery of sin to the freedom of the Spirit, from self to Jesus, from the imperfect world of multiplicity, confusion, and appearances to the perfect reality and eternal unity of God in the Trinity. But the phrase "Ladder of Perfection" or *Scalis Perfeccionis*, as it is called in its Latin transcription, never occurs in the text itself. The title here, *Coming to Perfection*, seems in the light of Hebrews 6:1 to capture somewhat better the language and theme of the whole treatise taken as one book.

What Hilton wants his reader to do, as we see, is to get beyond the simple "principles of the doctrine of Christ," the essentials of faith, and to begin the arduous but deeply rewarding process of growth in Christ. In apostolic terms, what he is asking is that we should not content ourselves with a self-congratulatory reiteration of the "foundation of repentance from dead works, and of faith toward God" (Hebrews 6:1), but to move on in an increasing desire of love for Jesus, deepening our knowledge of him and with it a self-perspective which allows us to order our spiritual priorities. As we do, he says, we will see how our love is to be "made perfect" (1 John 4:17) and how it is that by grace we are to focus all our being upon him, until "we all come in the unity of the faith, and of the knowledge of the Son of God, unto a perfect man, unto the measure of the stature of the fulness of Christ" (Ephesians 4:13).

The governing image in Hilton's examination is that of the soul as *imago dei*—created in the image of God. This image, which originally granted us a fullness of communion, has been damaged severely by sin—both original and personal, active and willful. It is, in fact, so overlaid with the negative image of sin that it is lost to us and must be sought after diligently. Hilton applies the parable of the lost coin in an exciting way, seeing it as a model for what we are to do in search of our own lost image. With the light of God's Word (Psalm 119:105) and the light of grace by his Holy Spirit, we are to sweep away the dust and debris of our lives until that treasure which he has intended for us is found. Then, he says, we can be truly merry and rejoice. Indeed, the special joy of that discovery turns out to be that the image we have been seeking is Jesus himself.

Hilton tells us often in this work that we need to pray for an opening of our spiritual eyes, so that we might have a less clouded vision of Jesus. He insists that our eyes are far from clear-seeing, that we are not only "dull-eyed" but even effectively blinded by an insistent imposition of our own self-image between our broken hearts and the health offered us in Jesus. How are we to obtain a greater clarity, he asks, except by dealing honestly with the complex and confused screen provided by our own ego?

When we first look for the image of God within ourselves, Hilton says, we will find, before coming to it, something far less attractive—what he calls the "negative image," or the "image of sin." We must first become aware of our own shortcomings, especially our own ingenious capacity for self-deception. We need to recognize in ourselves, moreover, not only the symptoms of sin, our "problem areas," but "the very root of sin," the latent propensity for sin which is universal. And when we are brought face to face with this dark image of ourselves, we ought not to take it as a sign that we are being defeated in our attempt to discover the image of God lost beneath it; rather, we should see it as a sign that our broom is getting down to the debris that most needs to be swept away.

Hilton is one of the great psychologists of Christian spiritual tradition. He is pragmatic, a spiritual realist. The "re-forming" of God's image in us by conformity to Jesus is not something he tells us will happen on a given Sunday night. Rather, it comes about as a process of spiritual growth. And this growth, if it is to take place, depends at each step absolutely on truth, on accepting the facts as they are.

This simple insistence on truthfulness is the very heart of everything Hilton has to say to us, as it is at the heart of the words of Jesus in the Gospel (John 14:6). For him, the Holy Spirit is indeed the Spirit of Truth (John 14:17). To the echo of Jesus' words "and ye shall know the truth, and the truth shall make you free" (John 8:32), Hilton is always asking his reader the implicit question, "What is it then that binds us?" All of us, to some degree, are shamed by the necessary answer.

There are two truths with which Hilton is principally concerned: the truth of the self and the truth of Jesus. "Soothfastness," as he calls it—truthfulness and integrity— demands that we see things as they really are, without fudging the picture. Pride in all of its forms—self-preoccupation, self-promotion, and self-pity among them—distorts and even destroys our vision. Only the person, therefore, who is truly meek can see through to Jesus, because only that person will have been able first to get himself out of the way.

Meekness is truthfulness, when we look at it in Walter Hilton's scriptural way. Pretension comes to us in so many subtle forms, continuously elaborating new ruses as we labor to protect our persona—what we think of as our identity—that only a total housecleaning, a candid search daily undertaken, will eventually see us to the bottom of things, to the unadorned, naked reality of our sinful selves. And because God loves us from the beginning, he grants us the light we need to get underneath all that surface clutter, so that in a meek acceptance of the truth which is ourself we are prepared, eyes opened, to find him and see him truly.

Self-knowledge and the knowledge of God are thus interdependent, Hilton says. We need to recognize who we are if we are to be able to appreciate properly who he is. Hilton's gauge for personal knowledge is a very simple one: "Man," he says, "is naught else but his thoughts and his loves." This idea, deriving from the Gospels via Augustine, is basic to Hilton's spiritual psychology: if we want to know what a person is, we have simply to ask what it is he loves, and how he loves it.

Applying this general principle in practical terms to his reader's own self-examination, Hilton says: "If you really want to know what it is you love, consider what it is you are most thinking about. For where your love is, there your eye will be turned, your pleasure found, and your heart preoccupied. If you love God very much, you will take your pleasure in thinking a great deal about him. If you love him only a little, you will only think about him a little of the time."

The right end of self-knowledge is the ability to accept the truths of our limited, feeble, and sin-prone self in meekness. That happens when, in honesty with ourselves, we are able to lay down the burden of our sin, our guilt and self-preoccupation, and respond to the invitation of Jesus: "Come unto me, all ye that labour and are heavy laden, and I will give you rest. Take my yoke upon you, and learn of me; for I am meek and lowly in heart: and ye shall find rest unto your souls" (Matthew 11:28-29). If we are ever to find rest and peace, it will be when we have found it in him, exchanging our own pack of psychological and spiritual junk for his clean yoke, his exemplary meekness and lowliness of heart.

This exchange is initiated when we enter into grace with what Hilton calls our "reformation in faith," believing the promises of God to be true and trusting utterly in Jesus for our salvation. At that point, the disfigured image of God in us begins to be reformed. But Hilton calls his reader to growth, to a further "reformation in faith and spiritual consciousness," an increase of spiritual maturity. While we may not be fully perfected in grace until we come to heaven, a clearer image of Jesus is possible to us even now.

Hilton is deeply indebted to St. Paul for what he says here. In one passage he quotes Paul's reference to his own charges as "my little children," and with Paul he speaks of "travail[ing] in birth again until Christ be formed in you" (Galatians 4:19). His object, like Paul's, is not merely to celebrate the state of grace into which we have come because of the gift of our salvation in Jesus, but to encourage a state of spiritual consciousness in which by the power of the Holy Spirit we are aware of the working of grace in us and keenly attuned to his ways of speaking to us.

What Hilton recommends his reader strive for is described in much the same terms by our own near-contemporary, A. W. Tozer:

> This intercourse between God and the soul is known to us in conscious personal awareness. It is personal: that is, it does not come through the body of believers, as such, but is known to the individual, and to the body through the individuals which compose it. And it is conscious: that is, it does not stay below the threshold of consciousness and work there unknown to the soul . . . but comes within the field of awareness where the man can "know" it as he knows any other fact of experience.[5]

Hilton keenly desires that his reader should come to a place where she is really possessed by love, that is, by God's Holy Spirit. He warns her against confusing the presence of spiritual gifts with the presence of the Holy Spirit himself; they are not the same thing, nor are charismatic manifestations a necessary evidence of his presence. Hilton is not advocating a subjective or introverted spirituality, but rather, as much as possible, a defeat of the temptation to introversion and self-centeredness by a steadfast focus on Jesus and meek openness to the Holy Spirit, which allows preoccupation with the self to be replaced by a true inwardness. This inwardness is founded upon restedness in Jesus, which is true self-abandon.

We can now see what Hilton means by his "double reformation." In the soul's progress toward perfection, the "reformation of faith" is conversion from love of the world; it involves being redirected, purged, and set on a new course. This is the place of all who are redeemed—at worst the state of nominal Christians, at best the place of Christians in a more spiritually disciplined lifestyle who have not yet quite approached the contemplative spirit he celebrates.

The "reformation of spiritual consciousness," which follows this initial reformation, embraces the two stages of spiritual progress spoken of by almost all the mystical writers, the illuminative and the unitive. The soul which experiences this degree of reformation of the image of God in itself is one which has left more and more of the encumbrances of the world behind, until there is greater and greater spiritual "space" for the Holy Spirit. At last, partially in this life but fully in the life to come, knowledge and experience are fulfilled in a clarified vision of Jesus.[6]

This, then, is what the contemplative life is all about. It is not so much a state of formal vocation that comes, as Hilton says, when someone walks into a religious house or community. Rather, it is a state of spiritual awareness open to anyone who will give himself to it utterly, knowing himself ever more truthfully as he looks more and more steadfastly upon Jesus. For that is the essential meaning of contemplation: looking upon Jesus.

HILTON'S CONTEMPORARY INSIGHTS

By this point it will be clear that Hilton's acute psychology, his profound scriptural insight into human nature, and his keen spiritual discernment all make of him a writer well worth our close attention today.

I came to Hilton myself by an indirect route. At a time in my life when I had begun to be discouraged with the very writers I had earlier admired, I found a little book by A. W. Tozer, entitled *The Knowledge of the Holy* (New York: Harper & Row, 1961). I read it intently, and quietly. Among the many gems of spiritual discernment, I found the words: "God constantly encourages us to trust Him in the dark" (69). Because I felt darkness, I was keen to read on. As I did, I noticed the many footnotes to medieval spiritual writers, men and women such as Richard Rolle, Dame Julian of Norwich, the unknown author of the *Cloud of Unknowing*, St. Anselm, Nicholas of Cusa, St. Augustine; the list went on. Indeed, in his preface Tozer went so far as to say that were Christians today reading such works, a book like his would have no reason for being .

What Tozer made me realize was that I knew almost nothing of the great spiritual writers of the medieval church, that the first 1500 years or so of the life of Christ's Body in this world had, as far as my knowledge was concerned, dropped like a stone into a deep well. I resolved to try to lower my little cup somewhat into that well, and when I did, found the water there to be refreshing, pure and sweet.

Tozer writes that "to have found God and still to pursue Him is the soul's paradox of love, scorned indeed by the too-easily-satisfied religionist, but justified in happy experience by children of the burning heart." Readers of Walter Hilton will recognize here deep affinities between the two men. And it is clear that Hilton, were he alive today, would be distressed by the same things that concerned Tozer, the "I found it" bumper sticker mentality that in its smugness has no time for the lover's ever-deepening desire for communion with the Beloved. Tozer puts it this way:

> Everything is made to center upon the initial act of "accepting Christ" (a term, incidentally, which is not found in the Bible) and we are not expected thereafter to crave any further revelation of God to our souls. We have been snared in the coils of a spurious logic which insists that if we have found Him we need no more seek Him. [7]

What Hilton, for his part, is telling us, in page after page, is that to know and love God is to seek him always, and to know that he is there, waiting to be wanted.

I turned from Tozer to the spiritual writers of the Middle Ages, and have spent most of the last twenty years in a growing appreciation of their insight into spiritual things. Hilton among them has come to have a special place in my heart, partly because only in the last few years have I been forced to the painful sort of self-examination he proposes. When he underscores the absolute necessity of truth with the self—a meekness that accepts the raw facts of life and does not try to color them for advantage or camouflage—Hilton speaks plainly indeed, and I involuntarily wince. When he says that our standards for loving our neighbor are shoddy and self-serving, and that the true standard for such love is Jesus' treatment of Judas, my heart sinks within me. Prone to judgment—probably because I am so open to it myself—I find Hilton's words about meekness to be an incisive thrust into the most vulnerable fabric in my armor. Who can understand himself, let alone his fellow Christian? Hilton answers that spiritual discernment outside of meekness is not possible. Who can love himself appropriately, or love his fellow Christian? "Only one who is meek, and nobody else can do it" (Book I, chap. 6).

Walter Hilton cannot be celebrated for great intellectual achievement any more than he can for being a great reformer or major theologian. To use Kierkegaard's apt distinction, he was not a genius but an apostle.[8] But it is just there that everything which is of value for us today is to be found. This labor of translation may, I hope, have some small place in reminding us all, as I myself have been reminded in the working, that to be an apostle is for all of us our proper vocation.

David Lyle Jeffrey
University of Ottawa

---

[1]*Mixed Pasture* (London: Methuen, 1933), p. 188.

[2]Wycliffe did not really begin to become articulate on the subject until 1378, and the Wycliffe Bible was mostly done by his colleagues after his death in 1384.

[3]See Alaphrido C. Hughes, *Walter Hilton's Direction to Contemplatives* (Rome: Pontifica Univ. Gregoriana, 1962), pp. 6- 7.

[4]Wynkyn de Worde was Caxton's immediate successor. Forty MSS of any work is an astonishingly large number from this period.

[5]A. W. Tozer, *The Pursuit of God* (Harrisburg: Christian Publications, 1948), p. 14.

[6]For further discussion see Conrad Pepler, O. P., *The English Religious Heritage* (London: Blackfriars, 1958), pp. 401 ff.; and Dom David Knowles, *The English Mystical Tradition* (London: Burns and Oates, 1961), pp. 102-105.

[7]Tozer, *Pursuit of God*, p. 15.

[8]Søren Kierkegaard's brief pamphlet, *The Difference Between a Genius and an Apostle*, appears under that title along with *The Present Age*, translated by Alexander Drû, with an introduction by Walter Kaufmann (New York: Harper, 1962).

SELECT BIBLIOGRAPHY

Primary Sources

Hilton, Walter. *The Scale of Perfection*. Edited by Evelyn Underhill. London: John Watkins, 1923. Reprinted 1948.

_____ . *The Ladder of Perfection*. Translated by Leo Shirley-Price. London: Penguin Classics, 1957.

_____ . "Epistle on the Mixed Life." In *Yorkshire Writers: Richard Rolle of Hampole and His Followers*. 2 vols. Edited by C. Horstmann. London: Swan, Sonnenschein, 1895-96.

_____ . *Minor Works of Walter Hilton*. Edited by Dorothy Jones. London: Burns and Oates, 1929.

_____ . "The Song of Angels." In *The Cell of Self-Knowledge*. Edited by Edmund Gardiner. London: Chatto and Windus, 1910.

Secondary Sources

Chadwick, Owen. *Western Asceticism*. Vol. XII. London: Library of the Christian Classics, 1958.

Colledge, Eric, O.S.A. *The Medieval Mystics of England*. New York and London: J. Murray, 1961.

Gardiner, Helen L. "Walter Hilton and the Mystical Tradition in England." In *Essays and Studies* 22 (1937): 103-27.

Knowles, Dom David. *The English Mystical Tradition*. London: Burns and Oates, 1961.

_____ . *The Religious Orders in England*. 3 Vols. Cambridge and New York: Cambridge University Press, 1948-59.

Milosh , Joseph. *The Scale of Perfection and English Mystical Tradition*. Madison: University of Wisconsin Press, 1966.

Pepler, Conrad, O. P. *The English Religious Heritage* . London: Blackfriars, 1958.

Sitwell, Gerard, O.S.B. *Spiritual Writers of the Middle Ages*. New York: Hawthorn Books, 1961.

Underhill, Evelyn. *Mixed Pasture*. London: Methuen, 1933.

LETTERS TO A LAYMAN

Here begins a little book that was written to a lord of worldly estate, to teach him how to govern his spiritual estate in ordained love to God and his fellow Christians. It begins by considering how a man who would be spiritual must first engage himself in the bodily experience of repentance and in dealing with sin.

FIRST LETTER
TO ONE NEW IN FAITH

Dear brother in Christ: There are two aspects of living in the community of the Church by which Christian souls may please God and obtain the bliss of heaven: the one is bodily, the other spiritual in character.[1] Bodily work is principally the province of laymen and women who lawfully make use of worldly goods and purposefully pursue the ordinary business of living. This is the appropriate emphasis for all young persons, new in the faith, who have newly come out of worldly sins into the service of God.

By discipline of the physical life we are enabled for spiritual effort. We need to be able to break down the inflexibility of bodily desires by acquired discretion and such exercise as may make the body itself supple and ready, so that it is not antagonistic to spiritual disciplines.

Bodily and spiritual exercise.

For as St. Paul says, as woman was made for man and not man for woman, so bodily exercise was made for the spirit, not spiritual exercise for the body. Bodily exercise comes first, and spiritual exercise follows, as St. Paul says (1 Timothy 4:8).

And this progression is only appropriate, for we are born in sin and corruption of the flesh, by which we are so blinded and confused that we have neither spiritual knowledge of God by the light of our understanding, nor

3

emotional apprehension of him through the uncluttered desire of our love.

It is for this reason that we are not able, at a single stroke, suddenly to move out of the dark night of this fleshly corruption into that spiritual light. By reason of our own unhealthiness, we may not soon bear such a light, any more than we may with our bodily eyes when they have long been deprived the light of the sun.

Bodily work is a necessary prerequisite to spiritual labor.

Accordingly, we must patiently work our way through a process. First we attend to bodily works busily until we are discharged of the heavy burden of sinful disposition which impedes our attention to the spiritual life. Then, when our soul has been somewhat cleansed of significant "visible" sins, it can be made ready for spiritual work.

Bodily works help to loosen the grip of sin.

By this "bodily working" that I speak of, you may understand all manner of good works that your soul does through the agency of your physical senses and bodily members. These may be done for yourself as in fasting, staying awake for good cause, and restraining your fleshly appetites by engaging in penitent actions. They may be done for the sake of your fellow Christian by the fulfilling of deeds of mercy, whether these be bodily or spiritual in character. Or they may be offered unto God directly, in your suffering various kinds of bodily discomfort because of your love of his righteousness. All of these efforts undertaken in truth and by charitable love please God; otherwise they are worth nothing.

Thus, whoever desires to be well occupied in spiritual work will find it appropriate and profitable first to be well assayed for a long time in this matter of bodily work, for these bodily efforts are a sign and witness of moral virtue within, without which a soul is not yet enabled for work which is fundamentally spiritual.

Endeavor first to break down pride in your bodily bearing. But abandon as well every selfish type of inward reflection, boasting to yourself, or making a laudatory personal inventory of your gifts and actions—any form of presumptuous or vain affection for the bodily or spiritual gifts which God has sent you. Break down also envy and anger against your fellow Christians, whether they be rich or poor, good or bad, so that you neither hate nor disdain them, either in work or in deed. Also break down your covetousness of worldly goods, that in the maintaining or getting or saving of them you do not give offense to your conscience. Do not break the principles of charitable love toward God and your fellow Christian for love of any worldly good, and see that you get, maintain, or spend it without undue love and vain affection for it, as even ordinary reason requires. As much as you are able, break down also those fleshly desires which show up covertly—when you are feeling sorry for yourself, or are too much concerned for creature comforts, food, or sexual pleasure.

When you have done all this, having worked well and tested yourself in all such bodily works, then you may by grace ordain yourself unto spiritual endeavor. The grace and goodness of our Lord Jesus Christ be your portion.

SECOND LETTER
ON THE MIXED LIFE
PROLOGUE

The grace and the goodness of our Lord Jesus that he has shown to you, withdrawing your heart from love and affection for worldly vanity and indulgence in physical sins, and turning your will entirely toward his service and good pleasure, now brings into my own heart many new reasons to love him in his mercy. Moreover, it greatly induces me to endeavor to strengthen you for the godly purpose and good working that you have begun, to bring it toward a good end if I may, principally as unto God, but also for the tender affection and love which you have shown to me, even though I am a wretch and unworthy.

I. Why godly desire needs to be ruled by discretion, and works of stewardship wrought in the order of charitable love

I know well the desire of your heart, that you greatly covet to serve our Lord in spiritual occupation entirely, without distraction or hindrance of worldly business, so that you might, by grace, come to a greater knowledge and experience of God and spiritual things. This desire is good— and as far as I can tell, of God—for it is charitable love, set particularly on our Lord himself.

Nevertheless, this good desire needs to be shaped and governed by discretion in its outward expression,

The desire for a strictly spiritual life is commendable.

7

according to the state in which you find yourself, for charity unruled sometimes turns into vice. Therefore it says in Holy Writ (Canticles 2:4, Vulgate): "Our Lord gave to me orderly charitable love, that the end of charity should not be lost through my own indiscretion." Just so, this charitable love and desire that our Lord of his mercy has given you requires appropriate governance for your pursuit of it. In order that you may perceive the appropriate measures, you should ask yourself certain questions concerning your degree in life, the manner of living that you have been used to, and the grace of virtuous life which you now have acquired.

I am, then, urging you to resist simplistic extremes.

But such a life is not suitable to everyone. Do not utterly follow your instinct to leave off all occupation and business of the world, for these are necessary, in fact, for your self-governance and provision for all others that are under your keeping. I mean, do not give yourself entirely to spiritual preoccupation in prayers and meditation, as if you were a monk or friar or any other man not bound to the world by children and employees as you are. If you were to ignore these obligations, you would not in fact be keeping to an ordinate and charitable love.

On the other hand, if you were to utterly leave off spiritual occupation, ignoring the grace that God has given to you, setting yourself completely to secular business and attending only to the active life with a totality of absorption like unto one who never left his devotions, what then? You would here also lose the proper order of charitable love. For your state, as a layman, asks that you attend to both occupations, each in its proper time.

II. How the life of Mary and Martha, mingled together, is appropriate to those that have leadership responsibilities

You ought to mingle the works of an active life with spiritual endeavors of a contemplative life, and then you will do well.

For you should at certain times be busy with Martha in

the ordering and care of your household, children, employees, tenants, or neighbors. If they do well, you ought
to comfort and help them in this; if they do badly, then
teach them to amend themselves and correct them. And
you should regard and wisely know how your property and
worldly goods are being administered, conserved, or intel-
ligently invested by your employees, in order that you
might, with the increase, the more bountifully fulfill
deeds of mercy to your fellow Christians.

For you, a
"mixed" life is
most appropriate.

At other times you should, with Mary, leave off the
busyness of this world and sit down meekly at the feet of
our Lord, there to be in prayer, holy thought, and contemplation of him, as he gives you grace.

And so you should go from the one activity to the other
in maintaining your stewardship, fulfilling both aspects of
the Christian life. In so doing, you will be keeping well
the order of charitable love. Yet, that you may not be in
doubt of what I am saying, I shall develop these points
now in more careful detail.

III. To whom the active life is most proper, and to whom the contemplative

You will recognize that there are three manners of life:
one is active, as in business; another contemplative, as in
spiritual service; and the third is made up of both, and so
is called the mixed life.

Active life by itself is the province of laymen and
women who are secular, worldly, and who will tend to be
superficial in their knowledge of the spiritual life. Nominal in their devotion, they seem not to feel as much fervor
in love as some others do; they cannot seem to get the
knack of it. Nevertheless, they fear God and dread the
pains of hell, and therefore flee sin, desire to please God
and come to heaven, and generally are in good will toward
their fellow Christians. It is necessary and expedient for
such persons to employ works of the active life as busily as
they can, in help of themselves and their fellow Christians, for they cannot do anything else.

A purely contemplative life is the choice of men or

women who, for the love of God, forsake all occasion of sin in the world, and of the flesh, and all obligations, responsibilities, and care of worldly goods. By making themselves poor and naked, down to the barest needs of the bodily sort, they flee from the governance of other men into the service of God. For such persons it is appropriate to travail and occupy themselves inwardly in order to obtain through the grace of our Lord cleanness of heart and peace of conscience by the rejection of sin and growth of spiritual virtues. For these reasons, then, they come to the contemplative life, the special purity of which may not be had without both great exercise of the body and continual travail of the spirit, in devout prayer, fervent desire, and meditation.

IV. How the mixed life is especially appropriate to pastors as well as to those with responsibilities of secular governance

The mixed life suits those with responsibilities for other people.

The third kind of life, which is mixed, is appropriate to men of Holy Church such as priests and others with pastoral responsibilities, who have care and governance over others— with respect not so much to their bodies as to their souls. For such people it is necessary at times to employ attributes and endeavors of the active life, in help and sustenance of themselves and others. At other times, however, it is necessary for them to leave off all excessive busyness and to devote themselves for a period to prayer, meditation, and the reading of Holy Scripture, as well as to other spiritual occupations, as they feel themselves so inclined.

But it is also generally appropriate to certain laymen who have positions of leadership by virtue of considerable possession of worldly goods, and also have, as it were, a kind of lordship over others to govern and sustain them. Analogous responsibilities pertain also to other relationships, such as the governance of a father over his children, an employer over his employees, or a landlord over his tenants, assuming that these have likewise received as a gift of our Lord's grace a sense of devotion and some inkling of spiritual calling. To these folk also belongs this 'mixed' life, that is, both active and contemplative. We may see that if such persons, placed in and charged with responsibilities they have undertaken, were to abandon entirely the business of this world (and the very abilities which ought skillfully to be employed in the fulfilling of their responsibilities), offering themselves ex clusively to contemplative life, they would not be doing well or keeping the order of charity. For charity, as you know, lies both in love of God and love of our fellow Christian, and therefore it is only reasonable that he who has charity should focus on both objects of that proper love, not exclusively on one or the other.

He who for the love of God in contemplation turns away from the love of his fellow Christians and does not care for them as he ought, especially those in relationships to which he is bound, does not fulfill the law of love. On the other hand, whoever obtains such great satisfaction from works of the active life and business in the world that, while claiming concern and love for his neighbors, he turns utterly away from the life of the spirit to which God has called him, such a person does not fulfill the law of love either.

V. How our Lord Jesus Christ and godly men in positions of authority have given us examples of a mixed life

Our Lord, in steering some of us toward this mixed life, put himself in the place of such persons, both those who would be pastors and those who are disposed to positions of secular responsibility, and gave them examples by his own manner of life that they should be able to pursue a mixed life as he did. At times he communed and mixed with people, showing to them his deeds of mercy. He taught the simple by his preaching, he visited the sick and healed them of their illnesses, he fed the hungry, and he comforted those that were in sadness. At other times he broke away from the conversation of all worldly folk, and of his disciples also, and went alone into the desert, or upon the hills, and continued there all night in prayers,

The example of Christ

as the Gospel tells us (Luke 6:12).

This mixed life was thus revealed by our Lord himself as an example to those who take up the estate and calling of a mixed life. What his life suggests is that such folk should give themselves to their worldly business in reasonable measure, and to works of the active life such as may profit the people who are under their care. His life also suggests that they should make time for giving themselves entirely to contemplation, in devotion, prayer, and meditation.

The example of godly churchmen This life has been the pattern for holy bishops and leaders of the Church, who had responsibility for both the care of men's souls and the administration of temporal affairs. For these holy men of God did not abandon utterly their appropriate administration or stewardship of worldly goods, nor give themselves entirely to contemplation, despite the rich grace they had in such contemplation. No, they often broke away from their own spiritual rest and refreshment, when they would far rather have still been so occupied, and for the love of their fellow Christians engaged in the demands of worldly business for the benefit of those in their charge. Truly, this was charity.

Thus, wisely and in discretion, they divided their habits of life into two emphases. In the one, they devoted time to the lower part of charity by works of the active life, since they were bound thereto by the obligations of their ordination; in the other they devoted themselves to the higher part of charity in contemplating God and turning their mind to spiritual things by prayer and meditation. And so they had fully charitable love toward God and their fellow Christians, both in the affections of their souls within and in the expression they gave outwardly through bodily deeds and endeavors.

Other men, who were only contemplatives and free from all such responsibilities, could have a fullness of charitable love toward God and their neighbors, but it was restricted to their souls' affection and not able to have an outward expression. It often happened in such cases that the more intense the spiritual inwardness, the less was their capability for outward deeds—for they needed not to do this, since it was not part of their calling.

VI. To whom a mixed life is most suitable; to whom a contemplative is most productive

But these godly men of whom I speak, both those who were ordained and those who were laymen, had the blessing of a fullness of charitable love in affection within and also in outward working of their devotion. This is the distinctive character of the mixed life. And truly, for one who is in a position of spiritual leadership, such as a pastor, or for one who has a position of secular authority, such as a leader in business or government. I believe that this mixed life is the best and most fruitful, as long as one is committed to it.

For others, who are free and bound neither to temporal administration nor to spiritual ministry, I imagine that a contemplative life alone, if they come to it faithfully and in truth, would be best and most fruitful, most fair and expedient. If they make such a commitment, it is my expectation that they should not then leave it of their own free will for works of the active life—unless, of course, there is a great need for the comforting of others in distress.

VII. Here is shown what life accords most to the one for whom this book was made.

By what I have said thus far you may, in part at least, understand the character of the various styles of life commitment, and which accords most to the state of your own life. And truly, it seems to me, this mixed style of life is the one most suitable to you. For our Lord has ordained you and set you in a position of authority over other men in considerable degree, and lent you an abundance of worldly goods to administer and sustain, especially on behalf of all those who are under your governance and your lordship, as you act in strength and wisdom. He has also, therewithal, afterward by his mercy granted you grace to

For you it is important not to abandon either bodily or spiritual work.

have some knowledge of yourself and a spiritual desire and recognition of his love. I think, then, that this life which is mixed will be the one best for you and most appropriate for you to work in.

What it calls for is for you to wisely apportion your life into two dedications, spending some of your time with one, some with the other. You know very well that if you were to leave the necessary business of your active life and be reckless, taking no proper care of your worldly goods, how they are kept or invested, and if you were to have no concern for those who work for you or your colleagues, just because you want only to give yourself to spiritual occupation, then you could not expect to be excused when calamity came. If you were to behave like this, clearly it would not be very wise.

What are all your works worth, whether they be bodily or spiritual, unless they are done properly and reasonably, to the worship of God and at his bidding? Absolutely nothing.

Bodily works serve the body of Christ, his church.

VIII. That we should use the mixed life as we direct ourselves both to Christ and to the members of his Body

If you believe this, and that you are bound to the way of charitable love in justice and reason, and suddenly you want to give yourself willfully to something else which appears more attractive, but which is not ordained to you fully, then you are not worshiping Jesus in wisdom. It is as though you were busy about worshiping his head and face, to array it in fairness and fashion, but you ignore his body, his arms and his feet, though they be all ragged and torn, and you take no care of them. In this there is no true worship, for it does villainy to a man to be fashionably arrayed on his head with pearls and precious stones while all his body is left bare and naked as if he were a beggar. Just so spiritually: it is no worship to God to adorn his head and leave his Body bare.

Understand that our Lord Jesus Christ is head of a spiritual body, the Church. The limbs and members of this body are all Christian people. Some are arms and some are feet, some are other members according to the divine needs and workings of the body. If you are devoting all your energies to array his head only, that is, to worship him by turning your mind to his Passion or his other works of manhood and mercy, meditating on him, all the while ignoring his feet—your children, your employees, your tenants, your fellow Christians and neighbors—and if you let them come to harm for default of your not caring and tending for them as you ought to, you do no worship to God. You may be making as if to kiss his mouth by devout prayers, but all the while in your blind passion you are trampling upon his feet and defiling them, inasmuch as you are refusing in negligence to care for those for whom you have undertaken responsibility.

So it seems to me. Nevertheless, if you think that this is not the true state of things, and that it is the fairer office to worship his head, being occupied all day in meditation on his incarnation—think again! Stoop down a little to other works and wash his feet, and be busy both in thought and deed about the help of your fellow Christians here and now. For this is something we all ought to do.

Truly, he will grant you more thanks for meekly washing his feet when they are foul and stinking beside you than for all the precious painting and adornment that you can make about his head by meditating on his incarnation. For the Lord's face is fair enough, and needs not much any decoration you can give it. But his feet and other limbs, that are your dependents and neighbors, are sometimes very poorly arrayed, and need to be looked to and helped by you, since you are after all committed to do it. For this sort of work will he grant you much thanks, if you will meekly and tenderly look after it.

Know that the love-service you offer to your Lord, or to any member of his Body as need and righteousness requires it, when you do it with a glad yet meek heart, pleases him truly. Let it be enough for you to be at the least degree and lowest estate of duty, since it is his will that it be so. And it seems to me, since he has put you in that state to work and serve other men, that it is his will that you should fulfill this work with all your might.

IX. That on occasion a lay leader should withdraw from spiritual exercises and give himself to fruitful business in the world

I say this not that you should merely do as I say (for I hope that you will do all this and more). But I would that you should do so gladly. Do not think it less noble to be away a proportion of your time from spiritual occupation, engaging yourself in worldly business, in good leadership of your employees and tenants, or in other good work doing all in your power to help your brothers and sisters in the Lord. Think rather that you should do both kinds of work in diverse times, each with a good will, as you are able.

If you have been at prayer for some period of time, break off now and again, and occupy yourself cheerfully and busily in some physical work for the benefit of your fellow Christians. By the same token, when you have for a season been outwardly busy with your employees or other men in pursuit of profit, you should break off and revert to your prayers and devotions, after God has given you the grace to turn to him. And in so doing, by the grace of our Lord, put away sloth, idleness, and superfluous rest that you allow yourself to excuse as legitimate contemplation, and which sometimes hinders you from productive and timely occupation in necessary business. In this way you shall be always well occupied, either bodily or in spiritual things.

X. How by taking an example from Jacob and his two wives we may govern ourselves rightly in the mixed life[2]

If you want to do well, try to do spiritually as Jacob did bodily. Holy Writ says that Jacob, when he began to serve his master Laban, desired Rachel his master's daughter to be his wife on account of her beauty, and that it was for her that he worked in service. But although he expected to have Rachel as wife, he actually took Leah, that other daughter, instead. Afterward he took Rachel, and so had them both.

Jacob's name in Scripture may be understood as signifying "one who over-reaches in sin" (Genesis 27:36). By these two women we may imagine, as St. Gregory suggests in his commentary, two types of life in the experience of the Church: the active and the contemplative. Leah, whose name suggests "hardworking," betokens an active life; Rachel's name suggests a "glimpse of beginning," or "vision of renewal," betokening the contemplative life. Leah was fruitful, but dull-eyed (Genesis 29:17). Rachel was barren, but fair and lovely.

Leah can remind us of the active, Rachel the contemplative life.

Jacob naturally courted Rachel for her beauty. Nevertheless, he did not obtain her when he wanted, but had first to take Leah, and then Rachel. Just so, anyone who is turned by grace of conviction earnestly from the sins of the world and the flesh unto the service of God and the purity of godly living is likely to acquire a great desire and longing for Rachel—spiritual sweetness in devotion and contemplation—because that is in itself so fair and lovely. Only in hoping to have this quality of life can he dispose himself to serve our Lord with all of his might.

Yet often when he expects to have Rachel—rest in devotion—our Lord suffers him first to be well tested and tried with Leah—that is, either with great temptations, or with worldly business, bodily or spiritually, in the assistance of his fellow Christians. And when he has worked diligently in this way, perhaps unto the point of being almost overcome, then our Lord gives him Rachel—a grace of devotion and rest in his conscience. And so at last he has the good of both, Rachel and Leah.

So ought you to follow the example of Jacob: take these two lives, active and contemplative, since God has set both before you. By the first and active life you shall bring forth fruit of many good endeavors in the aid of the Body of Christ. And by the other you shall be made bright and clean as you behold that majestic radiance that is God's alone, he who is both the beginning and the end of all that is made.

And then you will be more truly "Jacob," not only one who overreaches sinfully, but one who overcomes sin, and afterwards, by the grace of God, your name shall be changed, even as Jacob's was turned into Israel.

Israel is as much to say, "one who sees God."[3] So if you are willing first to be Jacob, you shall after be Israel—and that is the place of the truly contemplative spirit. For God will either deliver you in this life and cause you to be free from your weight of responsibilities and business obligations, or else afterward, in heaven, he will bring you fully into the blissful presence of his countenance.

XI. That contemplation should be an object of our desire, and works of our active life pursued without anger or undue coercion

Your active obligations are important to God. A contemplative quality of life is fair and fruitful, and therefore it is appropriate to have it always in your desire. But you shall be in actual practice of the active life most of the time, for it is both necessary and expedient. Therefore, if you are interrupted in your devotions by your children, employees, or even by any of your neighbors, whether for their need or simply because they have come to you sincerely and in good faith, do not be angry with them, or heavy handed, or worried—as if God would be angry with you that you have left him for some other thing—for this is inappropriate, and misunderstands God's purposes.

Instead, lightly leave off your devotions, whether it be prayers or meditation, and go do your duty and service to your fellows, as readily as if Christ himself had just bid you do so. Suffer the interruption meekly, for the sake of his love, and without grouching if you can manage it, and let not your heart be troubled because of this intrusion of small business.

XII. That necessary duties kindle and tutor spiritual desires

It can happen sometimes that the more troubled you have been with the pressure of outward duties, the more burning the desire you have toward God, and the more clear then is your insight into spiritual things, by the

Lord's grace, when you come to your devotions. It is in this respect a little like when you take a lump of coal and want to make a fire with it. First you lay sticks of wood against it, covering the coal, and though it might seem for a while that you are actually extinguishing the coal with the pieces of wood, nevertheless when you have been patient awhile and blown on it, up springs suddenly a great flame of fire, as the sticks are ignited.

Just so spiritually, the will and desire you have toward God is like a little coal of fire in your soul. It gives you a certain amount of spiritual heat and even light, but it is quite little, and threatens to grow cold in idleness and want of fuel. At that point it is good that you should put against it some sticks of wood—good labors of the active life. And if it seems that for a time these duties shroud or overshadow the coal of your desire, that it does not burn as cleanly and fervently as you would want, then do not be fearful, but rather be patient awhile.

Active works can, in fact, enhance your devotional life.

Then blow at the fire—after doing your proper duties and service, go alone to your prayer and meditation, and lift up your heart to God, praying him of his goodness that he will accept the work that you have done as unto his pleasure.

XIII. How by humble, ordinary good works the love of God is nourished in many hearts

Hold these things as nothing in your own sight—sticks of wood—valuable only in his mercy. Be meekly aware of your own wretchedness and frailties, and attribute all your good efforts sincerely to him, inasmuch as they are good. Inasmuch as any of your work is bad, having been done without the circumstance appropriate to good deeds, whether by your default or want of discretion, then put the blame on yourself.

In this spirit of humble work shall all your deeds turn into a flame of fire, as these sticks of wood laid against the coal. In this way good work of your outward life shall not

Kindling for the fire of love

at all hinder your devotion, but increase it.

Our Lord says in Holy Scripture: "And the fire upon my altar shall be burning in it; it shall not be put out: and the priest shall burn wood on it every morning. . . . The fire shall be ever burning upon the altar; it shall not go out" (Leviticus 6:12, 13). This fire is love and desire toward God within the soul which needs to be nourished and kept by the laying on of sticks of wood so that it does not go out. These 'sticks' are of diverse materials, some of one kind of tree, some another.

For a man or a woman who is educated and has some understanding of the Holy Scriptures, if he has this fire of devotion in his heart, it will be good to gather some such sticks from Holy Scripture and so nourish that fire. Another person who is unlettered may not have at his hand the Scriptures and theological commentaries, and therefore it will be necessary for him to concentrate more on external deeds to his Christian brethren, so to kindle the fire, thus exercising the love of God for them.

And so it is good that each person, according to his station and ability, acquire fuel of one sort or another— whether from prayer, from meditation, from reading in the Scriptures, or from the exercise of charitable love in good work—so to nourish the desire of love in his soul that it does not go out. For the affection of love is tender, and can easily go out and vanish away, unless it is well kept and nourished by vigorous bodily and spiritual attention.

XIV. How the fire of love burns up sin

Now then, our Lord has put into your heart a little spark of this blessed fire—that is, himself. Scripture says, "Our God is a consuming fire" (Deuteronomy 4:24; Hebrews 12:29)—for as a physical fire consumes physical fuel that may be burned, just so spiritual fire, that is of God, consumes all manner of sin wherever it reaches, and therefore our Lord is likened to a consuming fire.

I pray that you will nourish this fire in you, that is, love and charity. This is the kind of fire that he himself sent into the world, even as he says in the Gospel: "I am come to send fire on the earth, and what will I, if it be already kindled?" (Luke 12:49). That is, God hath sent a fire of love, a good desire and great will to please him, into the human soul. And this is his purpose, that this fire should be recognized, preserved, nourished, and strengthened, for it is sent for our salvation.

The more desire that you have toward him, the more is this fire of love within you. The less this desire is present, the less then is the fire. The measure of this desire, in yourself or anyone else, is not recognized by the person himself, nor can you discern it, but only God that gives it. And therefore do not set out to strive with yourself in an attempt to analyze and measure how much of this desire you possess. Instead, be busy to desire as keenly as is possible to you the love of God, but not to take the measure of your own ardor.

St. Augustine says that the life of each Christian is a continual expression of desire toward God. And that is a great virtue, for it is the voice of the heart crying out in the ears of God. The more you yearn for him the more audible will be your heart's cry; the same will be true as you pray more effectively and think more wisely.

XV. The character of spiritual desire

And what is this desire? Truly, nothing but a loathing of all worldly pleasures and fleshly delight in your heart, and a fulsome longing and yearning trust for heavenly joy and the endless bliss of God's presence. This, in my view, may be thought of as the true character of desire for God.

Desire for God should undergird all your work.

If you have this desire, as I sincerely hope you do, I pray you to guard it well and nourish it wisely. When you pray, or when you are thinking, make this desire the beginning and final intention of all your work. Seek and nourish this only, and seek not after any emotional or physical feeling, nor any sensible sweetness of devotion, nor special visions of angels or the Lord in his earthly body, for these are not actually such a great matter.

Instead, let all your diligence be really and truly to

perceive, and find in your soul, and above all in your will, a proper distaste for all manner of sinful living, and strive for a kind of spiritual insight, a perception of the truly ugly nature of these things which surround us. Then you are more likely to develop a mighty desire for virtue, meekness, charity— in short, a godly life which leads at last to the actual bliss of heaven.

This, in my thinking, is appropriate spiritual comfort and sweetness to the soul. What you want is a clear conscience, free from worldly wickedness and vanity, and with that the possession of stable truth, meek hope, and a fullness of desire for the things of God. However you are provided with other pleasures and creature comforts, this is the one sweetness that is true, sound, and secure. And you will find it only where there is clear conscience, a vigorous rejection of sin, and desire and a taste for spiritual things. Any other comforts or sweetness, or any other manner of emotion, no matter how garnered, unless it leads toward this end and purpose is unworthy of your trust.

XVI. The difference between our desire and the love of God

This desire is an apprehension of our final union with God.

But now you may well ask whether this same desire can be called the love of God. My answer to this is that this desire in itself is not properly love, but a beginning and a taste for love. For love is properly a complete union of the lover and the beloved—one flesh; so God and a soul become, as it were, one in spirit. But such perfect union may not be realized in this life—only apprehended by desire and longing.

If one of us loves another that is absent, he greatly desires the other's presence in order that he may have the full benefit of his love and affection. It is just the same spiritually. As long as we are in this present life, our Lord is absent from us, in the sense that we may neither see him nor feel him as he is, and to that extent we are unable to have here a full experience of his love and affection. However, we may well have a desire and great yearning to be present with him, to see him in glory, and to be fully joined to him in love.

This desire, then, we may have by his gift of grace in our present life. In fact, it is by the gift of this implanted desire that we may be saved, for it is an expression of love unto him such as we can have in our present condition. Thus St. Paul tells us: "Therefore we are always confident, knowing that, whilst we are at home in the body, we are absent from the Lord. For we walk by faith, not by sight. We are . . . willing rather to be absent from the body, and present with the Lord. Wherefore we labour, that whether present or absent, we may be accepted of him" (2 Corinthians 5:6-9).

St. Paul says that as long as we are in this body we are pilgrims[4] from our Lord. That is, we are absent from heaven in a kind of exile. As such, we live by faith, and not in sight of him as he really is. We live in a knowledge of the truth, and not by emotions. We grow courageous, and have a good will rather to be absent from the body and present with the Lord; that is, we are made bold by a clear conscience and the secure truth of our salvation in him.

Nevertheless, as we may not yet be with him, therefore we strive with all our might, whether "present" or "absent," to please him, working to counter sins of the world and illicit pleasures with our desire of him and his goodness, allowing all things that would hinder us in our coming to him to be burned up in the desire of him which he has implanted in us.

XVII. How desire exhibits itself in action

You might also wonder whether it is possible for a person to contain this desire indefinitely within his own heart. And I imagine you doubt that this is possible.

As for myself, I suspect that you might have this desire within, at least with respect to intention and habit of mind, but not necessarily have the experience of acting upon it. For example, if you are sick, you have, as does everyone in such a case, a continuous natural desire for your bodily health. But however intense this desire might be, whether in your sleep or your waking mind, if your actual mental preoccupation is somewhere else, fastened on some worldly thing or other, the desire remains at the level of habit of mind: it has not yet the experience of an actual outworking. But when you think about your physical illness, meditate upon it or analyze it or consider thoughtfully the character of your good health, then you have an experience of acting upon your desire for health.

True desire for God always seeks an active expression.

The same distinction applies spiritually, in your desire for God. He who by the gift of God has this desire within, even if he is asleep or is preoccupied with thinking about something or other, he nevertheless still has this desire as a habit of soul—unless he becomes engaged in mortal sin. But if he thinks on God or on the means of a purer life or on the joys of heaven, then his desire toward God has an actual experience of outworking. As long as he guards his thoughts and intentions so that they may please God by prayer, meditation, or any other good work of the active life, then his desire is achieving expression.

Accordingly, it is good for us, in whatever business we find ourselves, to direct our desire to the Lord, and wisely act upon it in practical ways, employing discretion, as we apply ourselves in one activity or another, as we are so disposed and God gives us grace.

This desire for God is the root of all effective service. Know then, without doubting, that whatever good work you undertake for God, whether it is bodily or spiritual, is an employment of this desire. Therefore, when you perform a good service, or pray, or think on God, do not be doubting inwardly whether you really have a "feeling" of spiritual desire or not. Your action exhibits your desire.

Do not attempt to measure or conjure up spiritual feelings.

Some folk are without sound knowledge in these matters, and imagine that they cannot be in true desire for God unless they are perpetually weeping or crying out to God with words of their mouth, or else in their heart constantly uttering expressions of desire. It is as if I were always exclaiming, "O Lord, bring me to bliss"; "Dear Lord, keep me safe"; or other things of this sort.

We should realize that such words are efficacious whether they are sounded from the mouth or formed in the heart, for their purpose after all is simply to stir one's heart in desire for God. But it should be equally clear that without any such words, one pure thought of God offered in love, or reflection on any spiritual thing—the example of Christ's life, the joys of heaven, or the understanding of the Scriptures—is far better than mere words. For an uncluttered thought of God springs from desire for him, and the more truly spiritual is that thought, then the greater is your desire.

Therefore do not be in doubt or internal struggle when you pray, meditate, or engage in some service or other to your brethren about whether you are experiencing desire for him or not. Your action speaks for itself.

Nevertheless, though all your good endeavors, spiritual and corporal, are a demonstration of your desire toward God, yet there remains a difference between spiritual and bodily endeavor. The actions and endeavors of the contemplative life are properly and by their nature an outworking of this good desire. Bodily or physical actions are not necessarily so. For this reason, when you pray or praise or think on God, your desire is more whole, fervent, and spiritual than is usually the case when you are engaged in active service to your fellow Christians.

XVIII. How after a night's sleep you shall enliven your heart with prayers and godly thought

Now, if you ask me how you shall protect this desire and nourish it, I will address myself briefly to this question. I want you, however, to understand that I am not suggesting you always use the same procedures as I do; rather, I offer them so that you may have, if need be, some general guidelines. I may not—no, I cannot—tell you fully what will always be the best pattern for you to follow. I shall only say to you something of what I think applies to myself.

After your night's sleep, when you want to rise up and

Begin your day with godly thoughts.

serve your Lord, you will first notice in yourself that heaviness of the flesh that resists you, sometimes drowsy in sensual appetites, sometimes filled with impertinent thoughts. But you should promptly organize yourself for prayer, or turn your mind to some good thought such as may quicken your heart toward him.

The first step in this is to put all your effort into turning your mind away from worldly vanities and from whatever vain imaginations may prey upon you. Otherwise you will not be able to feel real devotion in praying aloud. And if you will be thinking of spiritual things, then do not allow yourself to be hindered with the intervention of thoughts about concerns of the flesh and the world.

There are many kinds of discipline of thought, and which will be best for you I am not in a position to say. What I hope you will do is work to discover that pattern of spiritual thought that will be sweetest and most peaceful for your devotional time, for that is what will be best for you.

XIX. How a rightful consideration of sin nourishes desire for God

Reflect humbly on your own and others' sins. You may, if it seems appropriate, sometimes think profitably about your own past sins and the frailties to which you are prone, and ask God's mercy and forgiveness for them. After that, you may also consider the frailties, sins, and miseries which fall to your brethren, bodily and spiritually, and ask God's mercy and forgiveness for them as tenderly as if they were your own sins and you had committed them.

Indeed, this can be a good discipline of thought, for truly you can make of other people's sinful experience a kind of precious ointment for the healing of your own soul. For although the material of which this medicine is made is in fact toxic, it forms a kind of paste alloyed with toxins, antidotes: poison to counter poison. As your own liability to sins and the sins of others are brought into prayerful juxtaposition in your mind, if you crush and meld them together with sorrow of heart, pity, and compassion, they will turn into a kind of ointment. This medicine can heal your soul from pride and envy, and in humility instill love and charity toward your fellow Christians. So reflect on this thought once in awhile.

XX. That meditation on the humanity of our Lord, wisely pursued, nourishes our desire for God

Also you may most properly have in mind the humanity of our Lord. Consider his birth or his passion or any of the works he did, and feed your thought with spiritual imagination of these things. This will stir your affection to a greater love of him.

This kind of thought is good, and especially when it comes freely as God's gift to you with devotion and fervor prompted by his Holy Spirit. Yet if it be that anyone is not readily and easily moved to an intensity of feeling in this way, I do not think it likely to be expedient for him to press the matter overly much, as if somehow it were an exercise over which one can simply achieve a mastery. He might almost break his head over it and never be the nearer.

Remember thankfully the gift of God in Christ.

Accordingly, I think it is good to have the humanity of Christ on your mind betimes, and if profitable devotion and a sense of the Spirit come withal, keep to it for a while. But do not overdo it either; break off after a season. And if by any chance your devotion does not become readily more fruitful by this kind of meditation, then do not strive overly much after it. Take as a gift what will come easily, then turn yourself to some other profitable thought.

XXI. That reflection on signal virtues nourishes a desire for God

There are other kinds of spiritual thinking, such as a contemplation of virtues. They include a recognition, by the light of your understanding, of what humility is and how a man should be humble. One may also come better

Consider the virtues you desire to be formed in you.

to understand the character of patience, purity, righteousness, or justice, chastity, sobriety, and other such virtues, and how one may acquire them.

By such reflection you are likely to develop a great desire and longing to possess these qualities in yourself, and
also to have a clear spiritual insight into the three principal virtues: faith,[5] hope, and charity.

By understanding and by desire for these virtues, one's
soul should acquire great comfort, granted, of course, that
he has grace of our Lord to enable him. For without grace
a man's thought is half-blind and bereft of the savor of
spiritual sweetness.

XXII. Reflection on the saints and their virtues nourishes our love of God.

Think also on the saints of our Lord, apostles, martyrs,
evangelists, and holy men and women set apart, and behold inwardly their manner of life, the grace and the virtues that our Lord gave them in their earthly lives. By this
remembrance steer your own heart to take an example
from them for better living.

Always direct your thoughts in devotion toward Christ. But much more than any of these, you ought to be
thinking of the soul of our Lord Jesus. It is he who was
fully joined to the Godhead, passing beyond comparison
our Lady and all other creatures. For in the person of our
Lord are two natures: that is, God and man, fully joined.
By the virtue of this blessed union, the which may not be
expressed nor even properly conceived by man's intelligence, the soul of Jesus received the complete fullness of
wisdom, love, and all goodness. As the apostle says, "For
in him dwelt all the fullness of the Godhead bodily" (Colossians 2:9), that is, the Godhead was joined fully to humanity in the soul of Jesus.

Remind yourself of the humanity of Jesus, then, in this
way: Behold the virtues and the all-excelling grace of the
soul of Jesus, and you will find that great comfort to your
soul. And also have in mind the power, the wisdom, and
the goodness of our Lord made known in all his creatures.

For although we may not see God himself here living among us, we may behold him, love him, and fear him, marveling in his power, wisdom, and goodness as we see these revealed in his works and his creatures.

XXIII. Reflection on the mercy of Our Lord nourishes desire for God.

Think also on the mercy of our Lord that he has shown to you and me and to all sinful wretches like ourselves, encumbered in sin, captive so long in the devil's prison. Think how patiently our Lord endured our sin, who might rightly have taken vengeance on us and condemned us to hell if his mercy had not constrained him.

Instead, for love he spared us, had pity on us, and sent his grace into our hearts, calling us out of our sinful condition. By his grace he has turned our wills wholly toward him and caused us for our love of him to forsake all manner of sins. Be mindful of his mercy then, and his goodness expressed to us in more circumstances than I can now mention. These bring into a soul great trust in our Lord, and full hope of salvation, and they mightily kindle the desire of love in our hearts for the joys of heaven.

XXIV. Comparison of the wretchedness of men and the joys of heaven nourishes desire for God.

It will not be beside the point to think also of the wretchedness, mischief, and bodily as well as spiritual perils that beset us in this life.

Weigh all that life offers against the prospect of heaven.

These we might compare then to the joys of heaven, how much bliss and joy is there; for there is no sin or sorrow or passion, no pain, no hunger, and no thirst; neither is there sickness, doubt, dread, shame, nor blaming; nor is there want of power, nor lack of strength, nor lack of light, nor weakness of will. But there is the sovereign fairness of God, light, strength, freedom, holy affections which will last forever; there is also love, peace, worship, security, rest, joy, and fullness of bliss without end.

The more that you reflect upon and feel the

wretchedness of this life, the more fervently shall you desire the joy, rest, and blessedness of heaven.

XXV. How the desire of worldly men and the desire of heaven are rewarded on the last day.

Many men, of course, are covetous of worldly reputation and earthly riches, and are thinking night and day, sleeping and waking, how and by what manner they might attain these things. Such folk entirely forget to remind themselves of the pains of hell and the joys of heaven.

Truly, they are not very wise. They are like children that run after a butterfly, not watching their feet, so that sometimes they fall and break a leg. What is all the pomp of this world, its riches or entertainment, but a butterfly? Truly, not more, and in fact, much less.

Therefore I pray you to be covetous of the joys of heaven, when you shall have reputation and riches that will last forever. For at that last ending, when worldly and covetous men perish, they bring nothing in their hands. All their fame and riches are turned into nothing except sorrow and pain. Then shall all those who have been covetous after heavenly things, and who have forsaken truly all vain worship of this world's goods (or else, if they had them, set neither their affections nor true love on them) abide in in the mercy of God. Having set their hearts on the fear of God, in humility and hope (and sometimes in sorrow), they shall then have fully the things they have coveted: They shall be crowned as if they were kings, and set up with our Lord Jesus in the bliss of heaven.

XXVI. Discretion is necessary in the exercises of prayer and meditation, in order to know when to pass from one to the other.

There are also many other meditations, more than I can say, which our Lord may put into a person's mind to stir the affection and the soul's reason to part with vanities of this world and desire the joys of heaven. These present words I share with you, not as if I had fully explored the range of meditations that may be in a man's soul, but just to touch a little upon some of the possibilities, in order that by this small token you may increase your understanding.

Nonetheless, I think these suggestions may be good for you when you are preparing yourself to think on God, whether you do this in the manner I have indicated before, or in any other manner. If your heart is dull and murky, and you have not much spiritual motivation but only the barest of desires and a weak will, and you would very much like to think on God but cannot; then I hope that it will now seem good for you not to berate yourself too much, or strive within excessively, as if you would by your own might overcome your spiritual dullness. For in so doing you might easily fall into more murky dullness, unless you were to be wise in your handling of the problem.

Therefore, in such circumstances I hold it most reliable for you to say the Lord's Prayer, an *ave*,[6] or your morning prayers, or to read the Psalms, for these things are always a secure standard and will not fail you. Whoever will cleave to these as patterns for his devotional life will not go wrong.

If devotional thoughts do not come easily, return to common prayer.

If you can by your prayer life obtain a spirit of devotion, see to it then that this devotion be exclusively in affection and desire toward God, with a spiritual delight. Be diligent in your prayers, and do not lightly break off from them, for often it happens that praying audibly obtains and keeps a fervent devotion, while a cessation of such praying allows the devotion to slip away.

Nevertheless, if your devotion in prayer brings to your heart some Spirit-sent thought of the incarnation of our Lord, or of any other thing concerning him we have discussed, then this thought should be allowed to interrupt your words. Then may you profitably cease from your prayer and occupy yourself in meditation, until that also passes away.

XXVII. How one shall compose himself in thinking of the Passion of our Lord Jesus

You ought, however, to be aware of certain things in your meditations, some of which I shall now mention. One relates to moments when you have been in spiritual thought or imagination concerning the humanity of our Lord or aspects of his life on earth, and your soul has been fed and comforted therewith. This thought is likely then to pass away by itself. Do not then be excessively determined to retain it still by force or mastery, for then it is likely to turn toward pain and bitterness.

Avoid excesses.

It may well be that such a moment does not readily pass away, but preoccupies your mind; for desire of solace you will not leave it go, so that it prevents you from your sleep at night or else from the good work you should be doing by day. This is not good. You should break off after a reasonable length of time. Indeed, sometimes when you are most loath to lose this kind of devotional moment, if you extend it beyond a reasonable time, or else to the discomfort of your brethren, you are not acting wisely, in my judgment.

A worldly man or woman who perhaps does not feel a genuine spirit of devotion more than once or twice a year would be in a different situation. If such a one felt, by the grace of our Lord, great compunction for his sins, or else was brought to think intently of the Passion of our Lord, even if he were prevented from his sleep a night or two it would not be a matter for concern, since it comes to him so seldom. But for yourself, or any other person to whom this manner of spiritual waking is customary (let us say every other day or so), then it is expedient to have some discretion about it and not follow each opportunity to its most extreme possibility.

I think it would make good sense for you to use this rule of thumb in whatever form of devotion you are in, that you do not hang excessively long upon a moment of spiritual intensity, so that it either prevents you from your meals or sleep or an injudicious failure of service to someone else. "All things have their time and season" (Ecclesiastes 3:1).

XXVIII. How we should scrutinize our thoughts and desires, and wisely use the grace that God has given us

There is one more thing you ought to be aware of. If your thought has been occupied with the humanity of our Lord or some other such spiritual matter, and you find yourself afterward seeking with all the desire of your heart to have a more profound knowledge or powerful feeling concerning his godliness, do not press at it too hard. That is, do not allow your heart to dally too long in this wish, as if you were expecting or even gaping after some peculiar stirring or wondrous feeling, other than the sort you have already had. You should not behave like this.

It is enough for you and for me to have desire and longing toward our Lord. If he wills of his grace to send us his special light to open our spiritual eyes to see and know more of him than before we had by common works of devotion, well, we can thank him for that. If he will not do so, because we are not humble enough perhaps, or else insufficiently prepared through a cleanness of life to receive his grace, then we should meekly know our own sinfulness and count ourselves well recompensed with such desire as we have toward him. With our common thoughts that may easily come into our imaginations—as of our own sins and of Christ's Passion—or else with prayers from the Psalms or elsewhere in Scripture, we should love him with all our hearts that he gives us that much.

Humility and discretion are essential to true devotion.

If you do other than this, you might easily be beguiled into a spirit of error. It is presumption for anyone by his own wit to press overly much into the knowledge of spiritual things. He should not, unless he feels an abundance of enabling grace. For the wise man says, "It is not good to eat much honey: so for men to search their own glory is not glory" (Proverbs 25:27). We may add to this that one who probes the power and majesty of God without great purity and humility of heart shall be burdened and oppressed by his own efforts.

And therefore the wise man says elsewhere, "Do not seek for things that are higher, nor search into things that pass thy strength" (Ecclesiasticus 3:22, Vulgate). This is as much as to say, "Do not seek high things that are above your powers of mind, nor rummage about in great things above your grasp and understanding."

By this the wise man was not at all forbidding us to seek after and inquire into heavenly things, but he certainly has suggested that as long as we are not properly prepared spiritually, we ought not to take it upon ourselves by our own effort and wit to pry into or try to get an emotional reaction from spiritual things.

Even though we do deeply feel things of the Spirit and have a great and fervent love for God—so much that we count earthly things as nothing and imagine that we are ready for God's love to forsake all the joys and wealth of the world—yet we are not ready by ourselves to pursue and behold spiritual things that are still above us. We will only become ready when our soul is made more discerning, sober, and stable in virtues through a process of time and increasing of grace. For as St. Gregory once said, no man is suddenly made sovereign in grace, but little by little he begins and by degrees he grows in grace toward the perfection he seeks.

Amen

---

[1]*Bodily* and *spiritual*: the distinction is between an active and a contemplative life.

[2]The Martha/Mary allusion, which is used in chapter II of this treatise, was often used as a basis for moralizing the story of Jacob and his two wives, Leah becoming a kind of Old Testament Martha, and Rachel a Mary.

[3]*Israel* means, we now know, something more like "God strives," but it is interesting to see that the medieval exegesis is in the spirit of the passage in Genesis 32:28-31, where Peniel means "seeing God."

[4]Cf. Hebrews 11:13-16. Medieval writers generally attributed the book of Hebrews to Paul.

[5]The Middle English text uses here the word *truth*— which is often used by spiritual writers to translate *fides* ("faith").

[6]See notes 7 and 8 to the following treatise, *Coming to Perfection*, p. 178.

COMING TO PERFECTION

Book I
THE SPIRITUAL LIFE

Salutation

To my spiritual sister in Jesus Christ: I beseech you that in the vocation to which our Lord has called you in his service you may know yourself well placed and standing steadfastly. And I trust you are working busily with all of your soul's energy, so by the grace of Jesus Christ to fulfill in the integrity of good living the estate which you have entered—in quality as well as in appearance.

As you have by your choice become dead to the world and forsaken it in the sight of men, let it also be that your heart becomes dead to worldly affections and worries, turned wholly toward your Lord Jesus Christ. For you should know well that an outward turning toward God without the heart following is but a figure and likeness of virtue, and not effectual truth.

Accordingly, it is wretchedness for any person, man or woman, to forget all the inward keeping of himself, and shape himself outwardly only a likeness of holiness—mere show in habit, speech, and bodily works. One who is always looking at other people's behavior, judging their faults, imagining himself to be something when he is really nothing—such a person beguiles himself. Do not be like this, but turn your whole heart along with your body toward God, and shape yourself within, conforming yourself to his image and likeness there by humility, by charitable love, and by other spiritual virtues. Then you will truly be turned toward him.

I do not mean to imply that you can turn toward him in your soul in a fullness of virtues on the first day of your conversion as easily or as simply as you can walk physically into a house of prayer.[1] Quite the contrary. I want you to recognize that the purpose of your body being enclosed in this vocational way is that you might mature toward a state of spiritual "enclosure," and that just as you are bodily closed off from worldly commerce, in like manner your heart may be closed off from carnal affections and fearfulness concerning worldly matters.[2] And in order that you might be helped in coming to him the better, I shall tell you something of what I think in this little book.

Therefore leaving the principles of the doctrine of Christ, let us go on unto perfection; not laying again the foundation of repentance from dead works, and of faith toward God . . .

(Hebrews 6:1)

I

TRUE SPIRITUALITY

The knitting and fastening of a person's soul to Jesus comes by a good will and great desire toward him alone, a yearning to have him and see him in his heavenly fullness. The more intense the desire, the more securely is Jesus knit to the soul; the weaker the desire, the more loosely is he joined to it. Accordingly, whatever spirit or emotion lessens this desire, and whatever would draw it down from the steadfast mind of Jesus Christ and from natural inclination upward to him, that spirit will unravel and undo the soul from Jesus. Such a spirit is therefore not of God, but of the Enemy.

On the other hand, any spirit or emotion or experience or revelation which increases this desire knits the knot of our love and devotion to Jesus more securely. Anything that opens the eyes of the soul to spiritual knowing more clearly, making the soul more humble in itself, this spirit is of God.

True spirituality is grounded in desire for Jesus.

Here you may see something of the reason you ought not willingly to allow your heart to rest or delight itself wholly in any bodily experience or emotion, no matter how apparently comforting or sweet, even when such things are good. Rather, you should regard them as little or nothing compared to your heart's desire and steadfast

41

thinking on Jesus Christ; nor should you set your heart too much upon these lesser things.

What you should always be seeking with great diligence in your prayer is that you might come to a true spiritual consciousness of God. That is to say, you ought to pray to be enabled to know the wisdom of God, the boundless might of our Lord Jesus Christ, the great goodness of him in himself and in his creatures. For this is what is meant by "contemplation," and nothing less may adequately define it.

The matter is summed up by St. Paul when he prays: "That Christ may dwell in your hearts by faith; that ye, being rooted and grounded in love, may be able to comprehend with all saints what is the breadth, and length, and depth, and height, and to know the love of Christ, which passes knowledge . . . (Ephesians 3:17-19). Be rooted and grounded in charitable love, he says, that you might know no pleasures of the ear or palate or any other physical pleasure except that you know and experience in all holiness what is the extent and endless being of God, the breadth of his wonderful love and goodness, the height of his almighty majesty, and the fathomless depth of his wisdom.

The Goal of Contemplative Life

The occupation of a contemplative person ought to be in the knowing and spiritual consciousness of these things, for in them may be grasped the full apprehension of spiritual life. This very occupation is the one thing St. Paul coveted for himself, saying thus: "Brethren, I count not myself to have apprehended: but this one thing I do, forgetting those things which are behind, and reaching forth unto those things which are before, I press toward the mark for the prize of the high calling of God in Christ Jesus" (Philippians 3:13-14). This is as much as to say that there is one thing permitted me to covet, and that is that I might forget all things which are behind or backward, and always be stretching my heart forward in order to perceive and to grasp the sovereign bounty of his eternal delight. Behind are all physical distractions, forward all spiritual truths. St. Paul wishes to forget all physical distractions that he may perceive truths of the spirit.

Now I have told you a little about the nature of contemplation for this intent, that you might know it and set it as a "mark" before the eyes of your soul, and that you should desire all your life long to achieve it—even partially—by the grace of our Lord Jesus Christ. This is what is meant by the "conforming of a soul to God," which may not be had except one first be re-formed and in a fullness of virtues turned toward love. And this begins to happen when a person loves virtue for the good it is in itself.

Many people possess virtues—such as humility, patience, charity toward their neighbors, and so on—but only as a matter of rational choice and directed will, having no love or spiritual delight in them. Such a person will perform virtuously, but often with grouching, heaviness, or even bitterness in the doing. Nevertheless, perform he does, prompted rationally out of a fear of God.

Virtue and motivation

Such a person has virtuous reason and a disciplined will, but no proper love or affection for virtue for its own sake. Yet when, by the grace of Jesus and by appropriate spiritual and bodily disciplines, reasons are transformed into light and iron will into love, then this person will possess his virtues in love. It is as if at last he has so well gnawed away at the bitter bark of the nut that he has broken through, and is now able to feed himself on the sweet kernel. Suddenly the virtuous deeds which were once so heavy a duty are changed into a sweet delight. The person now rejoices in meekness, patience, purity, sobriety, and charity as he would in any delightful thing.

Truly, until our attitude toward a virtuous life be transformed to a feeling of real affection, we may have a secondary sort of contemplation, but the highest part of it will remain beyond our grasp. Yet since the practice of certain virtues helps to dispose us to true contemplation, then it behooves us to use certain worthy means to develop these virtues.

The means of
contemplation:
Scripture, medita-
tion, and prayer There are three means that people generally employ in offering themselves to contemplation. These are: 1) the reading of Holy Scripture and the teaching of godly authors; 2) spiritual meditation; and 3) effectual fervent prayer. Now, I realize that the reading of Holy Scripture is not readily available to you just now[3] so that therefore it is more appropriate that you should occupy yourself in prayer and meditation. By meditation you will be able to see just how much you yet lack in spiritual virtues, and by prayer you shall be enabled to receive them.

By meditation we learn to perceive our wretchedness, sins, and wickedness—such things as pride, covetousness, gluttony, and lechery, and the stirrings of envy, short temper, hatred, self-pity, grudging, bitterness, sloth, and unreasonable heaviness of spirit. When you meditate you will also come to see in your heart false humility and inordinate worry about the flesh and the world. These, of course, are the very feelings and emotions which are perpetually boiling out of your heart as water courses out from the spring of a polluted well, and they prevent clear sight of your soul, so that you may neither perceive nor experience clearly the love of Jesus Christ.

Know this well: that until your heart is substantially cleansed from sin—through the application of stable truth with respect to your own life on the one hand, and a diligent beholding of Christ's life on the other—you may not have a spiritual knowing of God perfectly.[4] Consider well the Gospel where he says: "Blessed are the pure in heart, for they shall see God" (Matthew 5:8).

In meditation you shall also perceive the virtues which are necessary for you to acquire. These may include meekness, mildness, patience, righteousness of heart, spiritual strength, temperance, purity, peace, sobriety, faith, hope, and charity. These are the virtues that you shall learn to recognize in your meditation. You will come to see how good, how fair, and how profitable they are. Then by prayer you will desire them and acquire them, for without these you cannot be a contemplative spirit. Consider the words in Job: "Thou shalt come to thy grave in a full age, like a shock of corn cometh in his season" (Job 5:26), and imagine that you likewise shall in an abundance of worthy physical endeavors and spiritual virtues enter at last your grave, which is the rest of contemplation.[5]

AN ACCEPTABLE SACRIFICE

In the first part of this reflection I have told you then about the goal which you ought to keep before you in your desire, and to which you should draw forward as much as you are able. Also I have spoken somewhat concerning the things which are necessary for you to make a good beginning, such as meekness, a secure sense of what truth is, and an undivided intent toward God. This is the foundation upon which you are to build your spiritual house, by prayer, meditation, and other spiritual virtues (Matthew 7:24-25).

Now I want to tell you something else. Whether you pray or meditate or do any other spiritual exercise, and in whatever degree it is good because of grace or bad because of your own frailty, and in whatever outward experience of your senses in feeling, seeing, hearing, smell, or taste or inward experience in your imagination or intellect: bring it all within the truth and ordinance of Holy Church. Cast it all in the mortar of meekness and break it small with the pestle of the fear of God, and throw the powder of all this in the fire of desire and so offer it up to God. If you will do this, I will tell you this much straightaway: that offering shall be pleasing in the sight of your Lord Jesus, and sweet shall the smoke of this fire rise before his face.

A spirit of meekness

What I am saying then is that you should bring all that you perceive and experience within the truth of Christ's Holy Church and break yourself there in meekness, offering the desire of your heart only to your Lord Jesus, wanting him and nothing else but him. And if you do this, I anticipate that by the grace of Jesus you will never be overcome by the Enemy. St. Paul is encouraging us when he says: "Whether therefore ye eat, or drink, or whatsoever ye do, do all to the glory of God" (1 Corinthians 10:31). So whatever you eat or drink or whatever kind of service you are performing, do it all in the name of our Lord Jesus Christ, forsaking yourself, and offering it up to him. The means by which you may do this, as I have said before, are prayer and meditation. First I shall expound a little to you on the subject of prayer, then of meditation.

II
ON PRAYER

Prayer is a most profitable and expedient means of obtaining purity of heart, the eradication of sin, and a receptiveness to virtue. Not that you should imagine that the purpose of your prayer is to tell the Lord what you want; for he knows well enough what you need. Rather, the purpose of prayer is to make you ready and able to receive as a clean vessel the grace that our Lord would freely give to you.

Now, this grace may not be experienced until you are tried and purified by the fire of desire in fervent prayer. For though it is true that prayer is not the cause of our Lord's grace being given, it is nevertheless a channel by which that grace freely flows into a soul.

But it may be perhaps that what you really want to know is how you should pray, and upon what things you should focus your mind as you pray. Also, you may wonder what forms of prayer are best for you to use.

THE SPIRIT OF PRAYER

As far as the first matter is concerned, in order to answer the question I would like to begin with that first moment of consciousness, when you awaken from your sleep. Though you are ready to pray, you will likely feel yourself to be sensually minded and drowsy, lapsing downward

Turn your thoughts wholly toward God.

47

into vain thoughts, either of dreams or fantasies or irrational imaginations of worldly activity or pursuits of the flesh. That is when it is a good idea to quicken your heart by prayer, and stir it as much as you can to a spirit of devotion.

In beginning your prayer itself you should not be setting your heart on earthly concerns, but all your effort should be directed toward turning your mind away from the world of things, so that your desire might be, as it were, stripped naked of even the appearance of worldly encumbrances, ever striving upward unto Christ. For you may neither see him physically as he is in his divine nature, nor contain him by a picture of his bodily likeness in your imagination.[6]

You may, however, through devout and continuous beholding of the meekness of his incarnate humanity, feel his goodness and the grace of his divinity. This may come when your desire is somewhat reshaped, aided and liberated from all carnal thoughts and appetites. And when your heart is mightily uplifted by the power of the Spirit into a spiritual apprehension and delight in him, and is held there continuously through the time of your prayer, you will have little concern for earthly things, for your mind will pay little attention to them.

Prayer as a kind of spiritual fire

If you pray in this spirit, then you pray well. For prayer is nothing if not an ascending desire of the heart unto God, with a corresponding withdrawal of the heart from all earthly thoughts. And so prayer is likened to a fire, which of its own nature leaves the earth and strives ever upward, ascending into the air. Just so, desire in prayer, when it is touched and lit by that spiritual fire which is God himself, is ever ascending unto him from whom it comes.

Not all those who talk about the fire of love well understand what it is. Indeed, what it is I cannot tell you myself, except this much: It is not of the body, nor is it experienced physically. A soul may feel it in prayer, or in devotion, and that soul will still be, of course, in the body. But it does not feel this fire by any physical sense. For even though it is possible that it will work so fervently in a soul that the body feels the heat, and becomes as it were burning for a sympathetic travail within the spirit, nevertheless the fire of love is not itself a physical sensation. It lives only in the spiritual desires of the soul.

Now this is not a matter of perplexity to anyone who experiences real devotion. But some folk are simple, and imagine that because it is referred to as "fire" it should be a physical feeling, hot in the way that a physical fire is hot. And it is for their sake that I am at pains to make the distinction.

TYPES OF PRAYER

Now for the second question, concerning what types of prayer are best to use: let me offer a considered opinion.

You should understand that there are three broad categories of prayer. The first is spoken prayer uniquely created for our use by God himself, such as the Lord's Prayer, and also, more generally, those prayers which have come down to us by the ordinance of his Holy Church—such as we have in morning prayer, evensong, and other services at their various hours. [7]

Common prayer. As for this first kind of prayer, which is also called vocal, or spoken, it seems to me that for those of you who have a religious calling and are responsible by custom and obligation for the saying of liturgical prayers, it is most expedient that you say them with all the devotion in your power.

Common prayer is profitable to those with a spiritual vocation.

When you recite your morning prayers, you say the Lord's Prayer principally among them. Beyond this, to stir your heart in faithful devotion it has been ordained for us to say psalms, scriptural hymns, and other songs of praise which are also authored by the Holy Spirit. Therefore you should not say them speedily and recklessly, as if you who are bound to say them got little personal benefit from the praying, but rather you should concentrate your affection and focus your mind so as to pray these prayers more soberly and more devoutly than any other special individual prayer. Know truly that since this is prayer which has been hallowed through use by all of Christ's Holy Church, there is no prayer so profitable for you to use vocally, and in community, as is this common prayer.

So, by the means of this kind of prayer, you shall put away all your heaviness of heart, and by grace turn your feeling of need into good will toward others, and your sense of bondage into great freedom, so that whatever burdens you bear shall not be able to hinder you in your spiritual life.

After these good prayers you may use others of their kind. Of them, choose those in which you feel most spiritual heightening and comfort: these things, in my opinion, should be discovered by personal experience in prayer.

It is also profitable for the new believer. This kind of common prayer is often also expedient for someone who is just in the beginning of his spiritual life, and more appropriate, perhaps, than any other type of spiritual occupation. For a new convert is still superficial, rude and carnal. Until he has a fuller experience of grace, he cannot readily think sound spiritual thoughts in meditation, for his soul is not yet fully cleansed from old, sinful habits. Therefore, I believe it is especially expedient for the new convert to use this type of prayer, saying the Lord's Prayer, the Ave,[8] and other prayers of this kind, and reading the prayers of the Psalter.

He who cannot run lightly in the path of Spirit-directed prayer, because his two feet (of love and understanding) are crippled with sin, will need to have a secure staff to hold him up. This staff can be those special spoken prayers ordained of God and his Holy Church for the aid of our soul's progress. By this type of prayer, the soul of a carnal person which is always stumbling down into worldly thoughts and fleshly affections shall rise up again, and be held to its course as by a staff. Fed with the sweet words of common prayer as is a child with milk (cf. 1 Peter 2:2), he may also be governed by it in such a way that he does not fall into errors or fantasies by immature meditations. For in this kind of scriptural prayer there is no deceit. Who so will, let him steadfastly and humbly learn to pray effectually in this way.

Let me add a note on this subject. You may have seen examples of folk who, at the beginning of their conversion or shortly after, as soon as they feel a little spiritual growth in love or understanding, but before they are yet grown stable, leave off spoken common prayer too soon. Sometimes they drop other compatible spiritual exercise as well, giving themselves entirely to meditation. They are not wise. For often in the tranquillity of their meditation such persons imagine and think of spiritual things according to the inclination of their own wit, and follow their emotions when they have not yet received sufficient grace to do so. By indiscretion they often outrun their wits or even break down the strength of their bodies, so that they fall into fantasies and singular conceits—even into open theological errors. So doing, they can for the sake of vanities easily abandon the grace that God has given them.

Common prayer disciplines the spiritual imagination.

The cause of all this can be a private pride and presumption. For example, some will, when they have experienced a little of God's grace, imagine that it is so extraordinary and superior to that given to others that they will fall right into the trap of vainglory. And so they will abandon the common prayer of all Christians. If only they knew how flimsy it is, this feeling of theirs about what God has given or may give to them, they would be ashamed to speak openly of it except by necessity.

We should all, then, remember the model of vocal prayer which David in this way offers to us in the Psalter, stirring us to pray in this way both with our heart and our understanding: "With my voice I cried to God, and with my speech besought the Lord" (Psalm 77:1; 142:1).

Personal prayer (vocal). The second general type of prayer is also spoken, but not according to any special model. This kind of prayer occurs when a man or woman feels grace of devotion by the gift of God, and in this devotion speaks to him as if he were bodily present in the same

Spontaneous intimacy with God

place. Here words are used which most accord with feelings at the moment of prayer, things which come to mind spontaneously according to sundry considerations which have been on the person's heart. This kind of prayer can involve the confessing of our sins and personal sinful disposition, or concerns about the malice and slights of our enemy; or else it may praise the goodness and mercy of God.

In this kind of prayer a person may cry out with the desire of his heart and the speech of his lips to our Lord, seeking his help and sustaining aid. It may seem almost like the voice of a man in peril amongst his enemies, or in sickness, showing his sores to the physician, saying as David said, "Deliver me from my enemies, O my God" (Psalm 59:1) or "Lord, be merciful unto me: heal my soul, for I have sinned against thee" (Psalm 41:4), or making other utterances like this that come to mind.

But this type of prayer is also well suited to a person who finds so much goodness, grace, and mercy in God that he wants simply and with heartfelt affection to express his love for him, giving him thanks by such personal words and psalms as accord to the loving and praising of God. As David said: "O give thanks unto the Lord; for he is good: for his mercy endureth forever" (Psalm 136:1).

This kind of prayer pleases God greatly, for it can only spring from affection of the heart. On this account it is never offered without some measure of grace. It is a type of prayer which belongs to the second stage of contemplation, as I have said elsewhere.[9] Whoever has this gift of fervent prayer from God ought when he prays to flee the company of others and get off alone that he might not be hindered in praying.

And whoever has this moving of the Spirit to pray, let him use it while he has it, for the true fervor of it does not last very long at a time. For if such a fullness of grace to pray comes in abundance, it is exceedingly taxing to the spirit, however exhilarating, and it takes considerable toll on the physical nature of those who experience it frequently. For when grace comes in such power, it makes the body sway back and forth in ecstasy, much like that of a man who is drunken and cannot steady himself. This is a focusing of the passion of love, which by a kind of violent overpowering breaks down all carnal appetites, wounding the soul itself with the blissful sword of love. In such cases the body may even fall down, unable to bear it.

This "touching" of the Spirit is of such great power that the most vicious and carnal man alive, if he were well touched once mightily with this sharp sword, would become serious and quietly sober for a long while afterward. And he would loathe all the appetites and lusts of his flesh, and all the earthly things which up to that point had provided him his chief delight. The impact of such prayer on the one who prays

Of this kind of experience in prayer the prophet Jeremiah seems to have been speaking when he said: "His word was in my heart as a burning fire shut up in my bones" (Jeremiah 20:9), for as a physical fire burns and consumes all physical things where it burns, just so spiritual fire, the love of God, burns and consumes all carnal affections and appetites in a person's soul. And this fire is well stoked up in my bones, says the prophet of himself. By this he means to say that this love fills up the capacities of his soul, his mind, reason, and will, with grace and spiritual sweetness just as marrow fills up the core of his bones. That is, the fire is within, and not produced outwardly by means of the senses.

Nevertheless this force is so mighty within that it strikes out into the body, so that all the body may quake and tremble. And because it is so far from bodily conditions which resemble it, and so unfamiliar, a person in such a state cannot control it by reason, and may not even be able to bear the force of it—falling down, as the prophet Jeremiah says, who was himself at last overcome in this way (Jeremiah 20:9).

Therefore our Lord tempers the intensity and withdraws the fervor, permitting the heart to fall into a sobriety of softness and tranquillity. But whoever can pray in this way frequently will be much blessed, and that speedily. He may acquire more spiritual growth in a short time The efficacy of fervent personal prayer than another, who is just as spiritually sound, obtains in a much longer time, despite all the disciplines of prayer that such a person may undertake. Indeed, whoever has this gift of God in prayer will not need to overcharge his physical nature with extremes of restraint and penitential exercise.

Personal prayer (silent). [10] The third type of prayer I have in mind is that which is only of the heart. It is without speech, and is experienced in great rest and quietude of the body and soul.

Habitual "soul prayer"

One who wishes to pray well in this fashion needs to have a pure heart. It comes to those men and women who, by dint of extended physical and spiritual effort, or such strong seizures of love as I have described, then come into a restedness of spirit. Here their affection is turned utterly toward things which have the taste of heaven, so that they may be in a state of unceasing prayer in their hearts, loving and praising God with a minimum of temptation and distraction.

Of this kind of prayer St. Paul has said: "For if I pray in an unknown tongue, my spirit prays, but my understanding is unfruitful"; that is, the mind is not fed. What then shall I do? Paul says, "I will pray with the spirit, and I will pray with the understanding also: I will sing with the spirit, and I will sing with the understanding also" (2 Corinthians 14:14-15); in the sweetness of the love and the sight of God he was thus able to pray. [11]

By this habitual prayer the fire of love should never be extinguished in the souls of godly men and women, which are an altar of our Lord. And let priests of the Lord each day lay to this fire fresh fuel and kindle it (Leviticus 6:12). Let the people of the Lord by holy psalms, clean thoughts, and fervent desires nourish the fire of love in their hearts, so that it never goes out.

EFFECTUAL PRAYER

Realistic goals

I can imagine that by now you are saying that I have been setting goals for your prayer life that are far too high, and that it is relatively easy for me to talk about such things, but much harder for you to do them. You may be saying to yourself that it is just not possible for you to pray so devoutly or in so utterly heartfelt an abandon as I am suggesting. When you would have your mind's eye turned upward to God in prayer you simply feel too many vain thoughts of what you have been doing before, or what you will be doing, or what other people are doing, and the like. You may feel that these things get so much in your way that you can experience neither the sweetness nor the restedness, nor even devotion in your attempts to pray. Indeed, you may be saying that often the more you struggle to keep your heart in a spirit of prayer, the more this spirit eludes you. Sometimes you can hardly concentrate in a time of prayer from one end of it to the other, so that you think all that you have been attempting to do in prayer is nothing but lost effort.

Well, as to your suggestion that I have been setting goals for your prayer which are too high, I am willing to admit that I speak of levels of intensity that I am unable myself to achieve. Nevertheless I say these things to this end: I want you to know how we ought to pray if we really are to do well in our prayer. And to the degree that we are unable to measure up, then we are humbly aware of our feebleness and may call upon God's mercy.

Our Lord commanded us to seek a totality of commitment when he said: "Thou shalt love the Lord thy God with all thy heart and with all thy soul and with all thy might" (Luke 10:27). It is impossible for any person alive to completely fulfill this commandment, yet our Lord commanded that we should love him in this way. St. Bernard suggests that he did so for this intent, that we should know by this standard the state of our own frailty and so be moved to cry humbly upon his mercy; and his mercy we shall have!

Let me tell you, nevertheless, what I think myself. When you pray, direct your will and intention as purely and completely toward God as you may in short compass of your thought. Then begin and do what you can. And

Above all, trust in the Lord's mercy.

though you be ever so frustrated in your first intention, do not be too much depressed nor too angry with yourself. Nor should you be impatient with God because he does not seem to be giving you that same quality of spiritual sweetness that you imagine he gives to others. Simply recognize your own feebleness, and bear it easily, holding before you your own prayer, simple as it is, with meekness of heart. And trust also securely in the mercy of our Lord that he shall make your prayer good and far more profitable for you than you know or feel.

For you should understand that you satisfy by this endeavor the debt of prayer you owe him, and you shall have reward for it as for any other good deed which you have done in love, even though your heart was not as fully concentrated as you would have liked upon the actual doing of it. Therefore do what is yours to do, and wait upon the Lord to do what he will do, and do not try to predict his response. And though you think yourself reckless and negligent, or in great default for your inadequacies in these things, just treat them like any other inadvertent sin which may not be entirely eschewed in this life, and lift up your heart to God! Acknowledge your failures, and ask him for mercy, with confidence in his forgiveness. And then stop struggling and stop being hard on yourself, as if you could by sheer self-control overcome your feelings of inadequacy.

Leave this off then, and go to some other good activity, bodily or spiritual, and set yourself to make more progress another time. And even if you fail the next time in a similar way, or even a hundred or a thousand times fail to reach your goal, yet do as I suggest, and all shall be well. And remember this: a soul that is never able to achieve real contentment of heart in prayer, but her whole life long is struggling with her errant thoughts and distracted and troubled by them, still, if she keeps herself in humility and love in other respects, she shall have a bountiful reward in heaven for all of her good endeavor in the Lord.

III
ON MEDITATION

Now I want to say a little about meditation as I understand it. You should recognize that in the matter of meditation there is no universal rule which can be established for everyone to keep in every situation. These things are, by nature, a gift of our Lord, and are directed to the various dispositions of his chosen souls according to their particular state and condition. And according to each person's growth in virtue and spiritual estate, he increases opportunities of meditation, both for their spiritual knowledge and love of himself.

For one who has always been ardent for the knowledge of God and of spiritual things, it can sometimes seem that he increases after a certain point relatively little in love for God. And that may be. But consider what is revealed to us in the life of the apostles. When they were filled with burning love of the Holy Spirit at Pentecost, they were not made fools or dolts, but they were made wonderfully wise—enriched in knowing and speaking of God and spiritual things—as much as any one might have in this life. And thus Holy Writ says of them: "And they were all filled with the Holy Spirit, and began to speak with other tongues . . . the wonderful works of God" (Acts 2:4,11). But all that knowing became theirs when they were being ravished in love by the Holy Spirit.

Meditation increases both knowledge and love of God.

57

There are a variety of meditations that our Lord puts in a person's heart. Some of these I shall tell you as they occur to me. My intent in this is your edification. If you experience any of these things, I would that you might more effectively take the advantage of them because of what I am teaching you.

THE GOOD OF MEDITATION

The contrite heart   In the first stages of the conversion of a person who has been greatly befouled by worldly or carnal sins, his thought is commonly directed toward those sins. With great compunction and sorrow of heart, great weeping and many tears, he meekly and diligently asks God's mercy and forgiveness. And if he is touched sharply because our Lord desires to purify him quickly, he is likely to be so overcome with the perception of his sins that he can hardly live with himself. And it can be that though he repent ever so sincerely, yet for all that he will still experience a kind of fretting and nagging of the conscience, so that he may even think that he has not properly repented and been cleansed from his burden. A person in such a state can hardly rest for his anxiety and travail unless our Lord of his mercy comforts him in such time as he wills. This comfort can be obtained by intense devotions or meditations on his Passion, or some other profitable meditation as he chooses to grant it.

In this manner our Lord moves in some people's hearts, more or less as is required. And all this is part of the great mercy of our Lord, that he will not only forgive our sins and trespasses but relieve also the purgatorial suffering for it, honoring what is after all such a little anguish of conscience.

We see that if God chooses to prepare someone to receive any special gift of his love, he first scours and cleanses that person by fires of compunction for all of his great sins previously committed. Of this kind of purging David speaks in many places in the Psalter, but especially in the psalm *miserere mei Deus*, "Have mercy upon me, O

God, according to thy loving kindness: according to the multitude of thy tender mercies blot out my transgressions" (Psalm 51:1).

THE GIFT OF MEDITATION

Some time after this sort of travail and wrestling with the effects of sin, such a person (or else another who by the grace of God has lived in relative innocence) may be given by our Lord a meditation on his manhood, or his birth, or his Passion, or his compassion for his virgin mother, St. Mary. When this kind of meditation is led by the Holy Spirit, then it is most profitable and an instrument of grace.[12]

You shall recognize it as such by this token or pattern. When it happens that you are stirred up to a meditation in God, and quite suddenly your thought is drawn away from worldly concerns and in their place it seems as though you are looking at our Lord Jesus in a bodily likeness as he was on earth, this is a gift of meditation. If it is suddenly as though you were seeing or reliving how he was captured by the Jewish leaders and bound as a thief, beaten and scorned, scourged and condemned to death; how lowly he bore the cross on his back, and how cruelly he was nailed upon it; or you see the crown of thorns upon his head and the sharp spear that stung him to the heart; and if in this spiritual vision you feel your heart stirred to such great compassion and pity of your Lord Jesus that you identify in his suffering in tears and weeping with every fiber of your being: then you will find yourself in amazement at the goodness, love, patience, and meekness of your Lord Jesus, that he would—for so sinful a wretch as you—suffer this much.

Identification with Jesus in his suffering

And if in all these things you experience a profound fullness of the goodness and mercy of our Lord welling up in your heart in love and joyful gratitude to him with many sweet tears, and you find yourself in deep trust that your sins are forgiven and that your soul is saved by the virtue of his precious Passion on your behalf, then you are indeed being blessed. For when the remembrance of Christ's Passion or any part of his human life is thus impressed upon your heart by such a spiritual quality of insight, and your own affection is responding to it, know for sure that this is not something produced by your own effort, nor a counterfeit of some wicked spirit, but it is a gift of God by the grace of his Holy Spirit. Here you will have an opening of your spiritual eyes into the life of Christ.

This may be thought of as a sort of corporeal love of God, as St. Bernard calls it, inasmuch as it is focused on the corporeal nature of Jesus Christ. And it is a great good, and of a major help in the mortification of serious sin, and a good means to come to a virtuous imagination, and so in time to contemplation of the Godhead. For no one can come to spiritual delight in the contemplation of Christ's Godhead except he come first in imagination by painful identification, by compassion and steadfast thinking on his humanity.

Consider the example of St. Paul. First he says: "For I determined not to know anything among you, save Jesus Christ and him crucified" (1 Corinthians 2:2). This is as if he said: My knowing and my trust are only in the Passion of Christ. And to the same end he says also: "God forbid that I should glory, save in the cross of our Lord Jesus Christ" (Galatians 6:14). And further he says: "We preach Christ crucified . . . Christ the power of God and the wisdom of God" (1 Corinthians 1:23,24), telling us thus that first he preached the incarnate humanity and the Passion of Christ; then he preached the deity of Christ and power and eternal wisdom of God.

IV
EXAMINATION OF CONSCIENCE[13]

Holy men of old have taught us that we should know the measure of our gift and exercise it appropriately; not taking upon ourselves to pretend to more than we possess in actual experience. We may surely desire the best of gifts but not always acquire the best, simply because we have not yet received that grace.

A hound that runs after the hare only because he sees the other hounds running will, when he grows weary, just sit down and rest or turn around and head home. But if he runs because he actually sees the hare, he will not spare himself for weariness until he has it. It is much the same spiritually. Whoever has a particular grace, be it ever so little, and he leaves off exercising it of his own free will so as to make himself work on some other gift which he does not yet have—largely because he sees or hears that others are doing it—he may perhaps run for awhile until he grows weary, but then he is bound to give up, to turn around and head home again. In fact, unless he is unusually wary, he may well scuff himself or injure his feet in pursuit of these fantasies before he gets back home.

The person who works according to such grace as he has been given, desiring by prayer meekly and persistently to add to it, and then afterward feels the Spirit stirring his heart to pursue the gift for which he prays, may follow

The hound and the hare: the folly of a merely imitative spirituality.

61

after it if he does so in meekness. Do not fear to desire from God as much as you are able for, or attempt to determine your own limits entirely. Everything that is part and parcel of his love is his to give. Whoever can most intensely desire God shall most intensely experience him. But exercise only the gifts for which you are able, and plead God's mercy for those that you may not actually fulfill despite your desire.

These are the sorts of considerations St. Paul has in mind (in 1 Corinthians 2:12; 7:7; 12:4-8; Ephesians 4:7) when he says to us that each person has his gift from God, "one after this manner, and another after that." For to each of us who is redeemed is given a grace "according to the measure of the gift of Christ." And therefore it is profitable that we should know the gifts which are given to us by God, that we might exercise them, for by those gifts which we have been given and thus made responsible for will we be sanctified, some of us by the means of considerable bodily penance, some by sorrow and weeping for sins their whole life long, some by preaching and teaching; and some by a diversity of gifts and graces of devotion shall be sanctified and come to glory.

RECOGNIZING OUR CONDITION

Inward evaluation   Nevertheless, there is a type of exercise in which it is necessary for us all to be engaged. And that is for a person to enter into himself, so as to come to know his own soul, its strengths and weaknesses, fairness and foulness. In this inward evaluation you shall come to see the honor and the dignity which the soul was intended to have by its original creation, and you shall see also the wretchedness and mischief into which you have fallen because of sin. From this perspective will come a desire of heart and great longing to recover again the character which you have lost. Also you may come to feel a great loathing and displeasure with yourself, such as is likely to produce a strong will to be excessively hard on yourself with respect to anything that prevents you from your soul's recovery to that originally intended dignity and joy. This is real spiritual travail, hard and bitter, especially for those who desire to make their endeavor quickly. For it is a travail in the soul against the very ground of all sins, great and small, which ground is nothing else but a false, misruled love of a person for himself.

Out of this selfish love, as St. Augustine says, springs every kind of sin, deadly and venial alike. Truly, until this earth be thoroughly ransacked, ploughed, broken up, and deeply cultivated, until it is really dried up completely in the weeding out of all carnal and worldly affections and fears, a soul may never spiritually experience the verdant burning love of Jesus Christ. Nor will it know the intimacy of his gracious presence, nor have a clear perspective on spiritual things by the light of understanding.

Preparing the garden of the soul

This is the proper work to which all of us are called, to draw our hearts and minds away from fleshly love and worldly appetites, away from vain thought and carnal imagination, and out from self-love and every destructive preoccupation with the self. Our soul should content itself in no carnal thought or worldly affection, for inasmuch as it is distracted from finding readily its spiritual rest in the love, the sight, and the intimate presence of Jesus Christ, it is bound to suffer. This discipline is pretty much a matter of the straight and narrow; nevertheless I find it to be the way Christ is teaching those who would be his perfect lovers in the Gospel, saying "Strive to enter in at the strait gate: for many, I say unto you, will seek to enter in and shall not be able" (Luke 13:24). You too must strive therefore to enter by a straight gate, for narrow is the way that leads to heaven and few there be who find it (Matthew 7:14).

Just how "straight" this way is the Lord tells us elsewhere when he says: "If any man will come after me, let him deny himself, and take up his cross and follow me. For whosoever will save his life shall lose it: and whosoever will lose his life for my sake will find it" (Matthew 16:24-25; cf. John 12:24-25). This is as much

The cost of discipleship

as to say: whoever wishes to follow me must learn to forsake himself and hate his own soul. That is, we are to forsake all worldly lusts and to deny the dominance of our physical appetites and vain affections, properly deposing the insistent demands of our sensual nature for his sake. And then he says: "take up the cross"—which is to say, "suffer the pain of this world's plight for awhile"— and then: "follow me"— which is as much as to say, "Look upon me. Contemplate me."

Indeed, this is a straight and narrow way, and no physical body may pass through it by itself, for it involves the slaying of all sin. As St. Paul enjoins, you are to "mortify your members which are upon the earth; fornication, uncleanness, inordinate affection, evil concupiscence, and covetousness, which is idolatry" (Colossians 3:5). So slay your members upon the earth—not literal members of the body but of the soul, such as uncleanness, lust, and unreasonable love toward yourself and toward earthly things.

Accordingly, as your effort has been up till the present to stand against great physical sins and open temptations of the Enemy, attacks from without, so it behooves you now to get on about the spiritual work there is to do within yourself. You need to be breaking up the very ground of sin within your own self, as rigorously as you are able. And that you might the more readily bring this good work about, I shall tell you more of what I have been thinking.

THE PSYCHOLOGY OF SIN

The soul as the image of the Trinity: memory, intellect, and will

The soul of man is a life in itself composed of three faculties: memory, intellect, and will. It is made in the image of the blessed Trinity, whole, perfect, and righteous.[14] Inasmuch as the soul has the strength and steadfastness to keep itself in remembrance without forgetting, dissuasion, or distraction, it bears a likeness to our Heavenly Father. The intellect, for its part, was made to be clear and bright and without error or muddiness of thought, as perfect as a soul in an unglorified body might have. Inasmuch as it retains any of this, it bears a likeness to the Son, who is endless Wisdom. And the will (or desire) was also made pure, burning toward God without beastly lust of the flesh or any other thing impeding it, given by the sovereign goodness of God the Holy Spirit. Accordingly, as it retains any of this character, it bears a likeness to the Holy Spirit, who is blessed Love. In this way the human soul may be called a "created trinity," and was originally to be fulfilled in knowledge, perception, and love by the uncreated Trinity which is our Lord.

This is the quality, estate, and dignity of the human soul in the nature of its original making. This is the state which you possessed in Adam, before the first sin of man. But when Adam sinned, choosing love and delight toward himself and lesser creatures, he lost all his honor and dignity, and you also lost this in him, falling from the design of that blessed trinity into a foul and muddied trinity of soul. That is, in Adam you fell into forgetting of God and inability to recognize him, even to taking on a beastly image, and that quite understandably. For as David says in the Psalter: "Man that is in honour, and understandeth not, is like the beasts that perish" (Psalm 49:20).

See now then the wretchedness of your soul. For even as your memory was at some point established in God, it has now forgotten him and seeks its rest in other creatures. Flitting from one to the other, it is not ever able to find full restedness, for it has lost him in whom alone full rest is found. And it is just the same in matters of the intellect. The will, moreover, which was once pure in its spiritual sweetness, is now turned into a foul and beastly sort of lust and affection, preoccupied with itself and with material things and sensual pleasures. You can see this happens both to your physical senses—as in gluttony and lechery—and in your imagination, which runs to pride, vainglory, and covetousness. This is so much true that it is hardly possible to do any good deed without its becoming contaminated with the instinct for vainglory. Nor are you readily able to employ any of your five senses purely toward the delectable things in creation without your

heart's being captured and inflamed with a vain lust or affection for them which puts out the love of God from your
heart, quenching both your consciousness of it and its actual sweet experience.

*The image fouled
by sin*

Every person who is alive to the spirit is well aware of
these things. This is the wretchedness of the soul's liability to mischief on account of the first human sin—let
alone all the other wretchedness and sins which we have
willfully added to it. And yet know this: even if you had
never committed any sin in the flesh at all, venial or
deadly, but only participated by your humanity in this
condition that is called original sin, it would come to the
same consequence. That is, you would have lost all of the
righteousness in which you were made, and would never
be able to be saved from sin's consequences unless our
Lord Jesus Christ by his precious Passion delivered you
and restored you again.

HEALTH: OUR SALVATION IN JESUS

*The Cross
covers every
transgression.*

It may be that you think I have up to now been sounding a little high-flown, and that you are not able to take it
all in or hope to live up to what I am saying. If so, I will
now try to come down to earth as low as you wish, for my
profit as well as yours. In this spirit let me tell you the
brunt of my meaning. Though you be ever so great a
wretch, and have done ever so much sinning, if you forsake yourself and all your works (good and bad), if you cry
mercy and ask only for salvation by the precious Passion
of Jesus, meekly and in sincerity, then without doubt you
shall have it. And from original sin and all other sin you
have committed you shall be saved.

Yes, you who are an enclosed nun—by this means you
shall be saved. And not only you, but all Christian souls
who will put their trust in Christ's Passion and humble
themselves, acknowledging their wretchedness, asking
mercy and forgiveness and the fruit of the precious Passion
only, humbling themselves to participate in the sacra-

ments of Christ's holy church. Even if they have been
weighed down with sin all their lifetime and never had
any profundity of spiritual experience or spiritual relationship to God, they shall in this faith and by their response
in good will be saved by the precious Passion of our Lord
Jesus Christ, and come to the bliss of heaven.

All this you may know well already, but I love to speak
of it. See here the endless mercy of our Lord, how lowly
he stoops to you and to me and all sinful wretches. Then
ask his mercy, and have it. Thus said the prophet, speaking in the voice of the Lord: "Whoever shall call on the
name of the Lord shall be delivered" (Joel 2:32). Everyone, in whatever condition or state, who calls on the
name of God may ask for salvation in Jesus and by his Passion, and be saved. Some folks respond well to this great
courtesy of our Lord and are saved thereby; others, believing in this mercy and courteous gift of God, remain still in
their sin and expect to have the advantage of it at some
future point that suits them. And then they are not able,
being taken before they know it, and so they damn themselves.

The mercy of
our Lord is
unbounded.

I know you are concerned at this point. You say: "If all
this is true, I am somewhat confused by what I find written
in the books of some spiritual writers. [15] I understand some
of them to say that whoever finds himself unable to love
the 'blessed name of Jesus' or find in the name spiritual joy
and delight, having by it a kind of transcendent experience of sweetness in this present life, will always be alien
to sovereign joy and spiritual sweetness in the bliss of
heaven, and never come to it. To be honest, when I read
such words they profoundly unsettle me and make me feel
very nervous. I have hoped, as you say, that many folks
will be saved by the mercy of our Lord, simply obeying his
commandments and following true repentance for sin in
their lives—people who have never had these ecstasies of
'spiritual sweetness' or 'indwelling savor' in the name of
Jesus or fervent love of Jesus' name. And so I wonder, in
the light of what you are saying, what to make of these
other writers."

To your concerns then I am able to say what I think, namely that when it is properly understood, the point that such writers are making bears the truth. Nor is it contrary to what I have myself been saying. For the name *Jesus* is as much as to say in English "healer" or "health."[16]

Now, every person who lives in this unhappy life is spiritually sick to some degree, for there is no one that lives without sin, which is spiritual sickness. As St. John says of himself and others who are being made perfect: "If we say that we have no sin we deceive ourselves and there is no truth in us" (1 John 1:8). And therefore it is clear that one may never come to the joy of heaven until he or she is first made whole, healed from spiritual disease. But this spiritual health cannot be obtained by the use of reason or the intellect, but only if one desires it and loves it, and has delight therein, inasmuch as he wants and hopes to get it. Now the name of Jesus signifies nothing less than this very spiritual health itself.

In this respect it is true what these authors say, that no one may be saved except if he loves and takes pleasure in the name of Jesus, for no one may become spiritually whole unless he genuinely loves and desires spiritual health.

It is just the same as the case of a person who is physically sick: there will be nothing on earth so precious or necessary to him, nothing that he will desire so much, as bodily health. Even if you gave to such a person all the riches and honor of this world, and yet did not bring him to sound health if that were also in your power, you would hardly please him. Just so in the case of a person who is spiritually sick and suffering the pain of spiritual disease: nothing is so dear, necessary, or so much to be coveted by him as spiritual health. And that health is Jesus himself, without whom all the joys of heaven could not please him.

This I imagine to be the reason that our Lord, when he took on human nature for the sake of our salvation, chose to be called by no other name—such as might have signified clearly his eternal Being or his power or wisdom or his righteousness. Rather, he chose to be called only by that name which signifies the cause of his coming, which was the salvation of men's souls (Matthew 1:21). It is clear that this salvation is most precious and necessary to mankind. And it is also what is signified by the name Jesus.

Then by this token it seems to be true that no one will be saved except he love Jesus (cf. John 14:6). For no one can be saved except he loves salvation above all, desiring to have it through the mercy of our Lord Jesus and by the merits of his Passion. And this love can be had by anyone, even someone who lives and dies in the simplest kind of faith experience.

It is also profitable for the new believer.

On the other hand, let me say that one who cannot heartily love this blessed name of Jesus in spiritual lightness of heart, nor enjoy it with heavenly melody here, will not possess or enjoy in heaven that fullness of sovereign joy which those who have enjoyed Jesus in an abundance of perfect charity in this life will know there (1 Corinthians 3:8, 14-15; 2 John 8). What these spiritual writers say may be understood in this way.

Nonetheless, whoever keeps God's commandments obediently, even at the simplest level of faith, will be saved and have his full reward in the sight of God (1 Corinthians 3:15), for our Lord himself says to us: "In my Father's house are many mansions" (John 14:2)—many sundry dwellings. Some of these are for perfected souls who in this life were filled with love and grace by the Holy Spirit, and sang praises to God in contemplation of him, with a wonderful experience of sweetness and a taste of heaven. These souls, in that they have had the most charitable love, shall receive the greatest reward in the bliss of heaven, for they are called God's "darlings"—his lovers.

Other souls that are not disposed to contemplation of God, and have not had that fullness of indwelling love experienced by the apostles and martyrs in the early church, these shall have the lesser rewards in the bliss of heaven, for these are called "friends of God." These are terms of

Friends of God

relationship used by our Lord in Holy Writ of chosen souls, saying: "Eat, O friends; drink, yea, drink abundantly, beloved" (Song of Songs 5:1).

Lovers of God   It is as if our Lord said thus: "You that are my friends, because you kept my commandments and set my love before the love of this world, loving me more than any earthly thing, you shall be fed with the spiritual food of the bread of life (John 15:14- 16). My lovers, you who not only kept the commandments, but also of your own free will lived in my counsel, and beyond that loved me only and entirely with all the power of your soul, burning in my love with spiritual delight—just as did the apostles, martyrs, and all other souls enabled by grace to come unto the gift of perfection—you shall be made drunk with the choicest new wine in my cellar." And this is the royal joy of his love in heaven (1 John 4:7-17).

V

REFORMATION AND CONTEMPLATION

Nevertheless, although all this is true of the endless mercy of God unto you and me and all
mankind, we should not because of our confidence in this become willfully more careless
in our manner of life, but be all the more diligent to please
him. Especially this ought to be so since we are restored
again in hope by the Passion of our Lord to the dignity
and bliss which was lost to us in Adam's sin. And although we may never obtain it completely here, yet we
should desire to be enabled to recover here in this life
something of the character of that dignity. We should desire that our soul might be reformed by grace according to
the image of the Trinity—which we had once by created
nature and shall afterwards have again fully in glory—
even if we are able to obtain only a shadowy reflection of
that image here and now.

This is the character of the life that is truly contemplative. It begins here in a consciousness of love and spiritual
relationship to God by the opening up of our spiritual
eyes. And this gift shall never be taken away, but rather
fulfilled and completed in the bliss of heaven. This is anticipated in the promise of our Lord to Mary Magdalene,
whose character was contemplative, when he said of her:
"Mary hath chosen that good part, which shall not be

taken away from her" (Luke 10:42)—the best part being the love of God in contemplation. [17]

I am not saying that it is possible for you ever to recover in the present life so whole or perfect a purity and innocence, or knowing and loving of God as you were first intended for or yet shall have. Nor may you escape all the misery and suffering of sin. Nor may you while still living in mortal flesh destroy and quench utterly that false, vain love of self, nor flee successfully all venial sins. Nor do I claim that these things will cease their tendency—unless they are stopped up by a great outpouring of charitable love—to seep out of your heart as does impure water from a polluted well.

What I want to see transpire is that even if you are not able fully to staunch this flow, you might become able somewhat to stem it, and grow toward a purity of soul as nearly as possible. For our Lord promised to the children of Israel when he led them into the land of promise (and so, in a figure, to all Christian souls): "Every place whereon the soles of your feet shall tread shall be yours" (Deuteronomy 11:24). That is to say, as much territory as you are able to tread upon with the feet of your desire, so much shall you have in the Land of Promise, that is, in the bliss of heaven, when you come thither.

SEEKING THE LOST

Seek then what you have lost, that you might find it. Well I know that anyone who once has an inward vision of something of that dignity and spiritual beauty which the soul had once by nature, and shall have again by grace, will loathe and despise all the happiness, pleasures, and beauty of this world as if it were the smell of bad meat by comparison. Nor will that person have the desire to work toward anything else, but night and day, saving the frailty and bare necessities of physical sustenance, will be desiring, mourning, and in prayer seeking how he may come again unto that for which he was created.

Nevertheless, since you have yet to see what it is fully, because your spiritual eyes are not yet opened, I shall offer you one word to cover all that it is you ought to seek, desire, and find—for in this word is all you have lost. This word is *Jesus*.

I do not mean the word *Jesus* painted upon the wall, or written with letters on the book, or formed by lips as a sound in the mouth, or as imagined in your heart silently by the work of your mind—though in this manner one who still lacks charitable love may find him. I mean Jesus Christ that blessed Person himself, God and man, son of the Virgin Mary, the one whom this name signifies. It is he who is all goodness, boundless wisdom, love and sweetness, he who is your joy, your honor, and your everlasting happiness, he who is your God, your Lord, and your Salvation.

So then: if you do experience a great desire in your heart toward Jesus, either by calling to mind this name Jesus, or by remembrance and perception of any other word, or in prayer, or in any endeavor you undertake: if that desire is so strong in you that it pushes out by its strength all other thoughts and desires of the world and the flesh from your heart, then you will be properly seeking the Lord Jesus. And when you feel this desire toward God, or toward Jesus (it is all one), and feel it being assisted by the power of the Spirit insomuch that it is transformed into love and affection, spiritual savor, and sweetness, and also into light and such a knowledge of the truth that for a time all else is obliterated from your thought, then you will know yourself in the right path. If you feel no stirrings of vainglory or of self-justification, or any other incommensurate affection, but feel yourself entirely enclosed, rested, softened, and anointed in Jesus, then you will have begun indeed to find him. Not that you will find him in his entirety, as he is, but you will find a true experience of him. And the more successful you are in finding him in this way, the more intense will be your desire for him alone.

Seeking Jesus only

Accordingly, by whatever manner of prayer or meditation or occupation you are able to have the most pure and intense desire toward him and the most profound consciousness of him, that will be for you the best way to seek him and to find him. So if it comes to your mind to ask what it is you have lost and should therefore be seeking, lift up your mind in the desire of your heart to Jesus Christ, even though in your blindness you may not see him in his Godhead. Confess to him that you have lost him and wish to have him again and nothing but himself, and that you wish to be with him. Tell him that you wish no other joy in heaven or earth except only him.

Seeking him always And even though you experience him in devotion or in knowledge or in any other gift whatsoever, do not content yourself in that as though you have fully found Jesus. Rather, "forget" what you have found, and always be desiring Jesus more and more, that you might discover him still better, almost as if you had not yet found him at all. For know this for certain: that whatever you might experience of him, no matter how much—yes, even if you were to be ravished into the third heaven with Paul (2 Corinthians 12) yet you would not yet have found Jesus as he is in his fullness of joy. However much you know or experience him, his fullness is far above that still. And therefore if you would discover him fully as he is in the highest bliss of loving, never cease while you live from spiritual desire for him.

The Value of Desire

Truly I would rather experience and possess in my heart a true desire and pure love-longing toward my Lord Jesus Christ, though I see but little of him with my spiritual eyes, than to have without this desire as much bodily repentance as all men alive. I would rather have this desire for him than visions, revelations, visions of angels, songs and sounds, savors and smells, burning sensations, and any pleasant physical sensation—indeed, than all the joys of heaven and earth I might have without this desire toward my Lord Jesus.

David the prophet felt much the same way, if I understand him. It was he who said: "Whom have I in heaven but thee? and there is none upon earth that I desire beside thee" (Psalm 73:25). It is as if he had said: "Lord Jesus, what heavenly joy is a pleasure to me without desire for you while I am in earth, or what is such joy without love of you when I am come to heaven?" And the answer is, nothing at all!

If you then wish to experience anything of him, physically or spiritually, do not covet anything except to feel honestly a desire for his grace and his merciful presence, and that you will come to consider that your heart may find its rest nowhere but in him. This is what David was coveting when he said: "My soul breaketh for the longing it hath unto thy judgments at all times" (Psalm 119:20). Lord, my soul covets to desire your righteousness.

Seek then, as David did, desire by means of desire. And if you are enabled to experience by your desire in prayer and meditation the intimate presence of Jesus Christ in your soul, bind your heart fast there so you do not fall away from it. Then, if you should stumble, you will soon be able to find him again.

Like David, desire more desire.

Seek then Jesus, whom you have lost. He will be sought after, and will be found. He says himself: "He that seeketh findeth" (Matthew 7:8). The seeking is hard work, but the finding is bliss. Follow then the counsel of the Wise Man if you wish to find him: "If thou seekest her as silver, and searchest for her as hid treasures; then shalt thou understand the fear of the Lord, and find the knowledge of God" (Proverbs 2:4-5). If you seek wisdom, which is Jesus, as you would silver and gold, and delve deeply after it, you will find it. It is right that you should delve deeply into your heart, for he is hidden there, and cast out completely all loves, pleasures, sorrows, and cares of earthly things, so that you will find Wisdom: Jesus your true love, and I trust, your Lord.

WHERE AND HOW TO LOOK

Parable of the lost coin

Try to be like that woman in the gospel, of whom our Lord said: "What woman having ten pieces of silver, if she lose one piece, doth not light a candle, and sweep the house, and seek diligently till she find it? And when she hath found it, she calleth her friends and her neighbors together, saying, Rejoice with me; for I have found the piece which I had lost" (Luke 15:8,9). What woman is there who, having lost a drachma, would not light a lantern and search her house up and down, looking until she had found it? We can imagine their answer: none. And when she finds it she calls all her friends over and says to them: "Make merry with me, and melody, for I have found the drachma which I lost."

Think of this drachma as Jesus, whom you have lost. If you want to find him, light up a lantern, which is God's word. As David says: "Thy word is a lamp unto my feet" (Psalm 119:105). By this lantern you shall see how to light up another lantern, which is the rational part of your soul, for as our Lord also says, "the light of the body is the eye" (Matthew 6:22). In the same way it may be said that the lantern of the soul is intellect, by which the soul may see into spiritual things (cf. Proverbs 20:27).

By the means of these lanterns may you find Jesus; at least you may if you take your lantern out from under its bushel. As our Lord says: "Neither do men light a candle and put it under a bushel, but on a candlestick: and it giveth light unto all that are in the house" (Matthew 5:15). This implies that our intellect should not be overlaid with worldly business, vain thoughts, and carnal affections. Rather, it should be lifted up above earthly concerns as much as is possible unto an inward beholding of Christ Jesus. And if you do this you shall begin to see all the dust, dirt, and small motes in your house, all the carnal loves and worries in your soul. Actually, not all, for as David says, "who can understand his errors?" (Psalm 19:12). And everyone must answer: no one.

And so you shall cast out from your heart all such sins, and vigorously sweep your soul clean with a broom which is the fear of God, and with water of your own tears wash it down. So shall you find your drachma, Jesus. And he is true currency, he is true coinage, and he is your inheritance.

This drachma will not so easily be found as the finding may be talked about. For the work is not a matter of an hour or a day, but of many years, with much sweat and toil of the body and travail of the soul.

Sweeping your spiritual house clean is serious work.

Yet if you do not desist, but seek him diligently, sorrowing and mourning in repentance until your eyes water for anguish and grief because you have lost your treasure, Jesus, then at last in his will you shall find him. And if you find him, as I have suggested—if in cleansed conscience you experience the intimate and peaceful presence of that blessed man Christ Jesus, an inkling of himself as he is in fullness—then you may, if you will, call your friends about you to make merry with melody, for you will have found your drachma, Jesus.

Consider then the courtesy and the mercy of Jesus. You have lost him, but where? Truly, in your own house—that is, in your soul. If you had lost him somewhere outside, that is to say, if you had lost all of your soul's rational aspect by that original sin, then your soul could never have found him again. But he left to you the faculty of reason, and so to that extent he is in your soul and shall never be entirely lost out of it.

But you are not any nearer to him, for all that, until you have actually found him. He is in you, though he be lost from you, but you are not in him until you have found him. Here then is mercy, that he suffered himself to be lost only in that very place where he might again be found.

You do not need to run off to Rome or Jerusalem to seek him there. Just turn your thought into your own soul, wherein he is hidden. As the prophet said: "Verily thou art a God that hidest thyself" (Isaiah 45:15). *Deus absconditus:* yet we may seek him there, in the soul. He says himself in the Gospel: "The kingdom of heaven is like unto

But the reward outweighs any sacrifice.

treasure hid in a field; the which when a man hath found he hideth, and for joy thereof goeth and selleth all that he hath, and buyeth that field" (Matthew 13:44). Jesus is treasure hidden in your soul. Accordingly, if you wish to find him in your soul, and your soul in him, I am sure that you will gladly give all the pleasure of the world to have him.

You might almost imagine that Jesus is sleeping in your very heart spiritually, even as he did bodily when he was in the ship with his disciples. Do you recall how for fear of perishing they woke him up and in short order he saved them from the tempest? Well, if you also are bold to stir him by prayer and waken him by a great crying of desire, he shall soon arise and help you. Nonetheless, I expect it is much more accurate to imagine that you are the one who is asleep than to think that he is ever asleep to you. For he calls you clearly and often with his sweet and still, small voice, stirring your heart gently, urging you to leave off all other jangling of worldly vanities in your soul to pay attention to what he is saying. Thus says David in the voice of the Lord: "Hearken, O daughter, and consider, and incline thine ear; forget also thine own people, and thy father's house" (Psalm 45:10). O daughter! hear and see and bow your ear to me, forgetting the people in your worldly thoughts and the household of your fleshly and natural affections! Lo! Here may you see how our Lord calls you and all others who will listen to his voice.

What is hindering you then, that you may neither see him nor hear him? Truly there is so much din and racket in your heart of vain thoughts and carnal desires that you cannot either hear or see him. Therefore put away that unrestful din and break away from love of sin and vanity, bringing your heart toward love of virtue and a fullness of charitable love. Then shall you hear your Lord speak to you. For as long as he is unable to find his image reformed in you in some respect, he remains estranged and far from you.

The imitation of Christ

Therefore prepare yourself to be clothed in his likeness, that is, in meekness and in charity—which are his own distinctive garments—and then he will know you as family and open to you his secrets. [18] Remember what he said to his disciples: "He that loveth me shall be loved of my Father, and I will love him and manifest myself to him" (John 14:21). There is no virtue or work which you may do which can make you resemble our Lord unless it have about it meekness and charitable love, for these two things are especially his characteristic style. And that much appears clearly in the gospel, when our Lord speaks of meekness: "Learn of me, for I am meek and lowly in heart" (Matthew 11:29). Learn of me, he says, not about going barefoot or going out into the desert to fast for forty days, not to try to choose for yourself disciples, but learn from me meekness, for I am mild and meek in heart.

And he says this about charitable love: "A new commandment I give unto you, that ye love one another; as I have loved you, that ye also love one another. By this shall all men know that ye are my disciples, if ye have love one to another" (John 13:34, 35). The commandment is not that we are to work miracles or cast out devils or preach and teach, but that each of us love the other in charity.

If you want to be like him, then have meekness and charity. And charitable love is simply that you are able to love well your fellow Christian as you do yourself.

Meekness and love

SELF-DISCOVERY AND THE IMAGE OF GOD

To this point, you have heard a little concerning the nature of your soul, what honor it was intended to have, and how it lost this honor. And also I have told you that this honorable estate, by grace and diligent effort, may be to some degree recovered again, at least in part.

Now I shall attempt to tell you, feebly as I can, how you shall grow able to penetrate your inner self in order to see there the ground of sin and to learn to eradicate it as much as is possible. So shall you be able to recover a portion of your soul's lost dignity.

Take time to pre-
pare your spirit.
You should cease for a time all bodily works, I think, desisting from external business. Then you ought to draw your thoughts inward, away from your bodily senses, so that you pay as little attention as possible to what you hear, see, or feel, so that your heart is not fixed on such things.

After this, draw your thought inward from all imagining, if you are able, of any bodily things, and put out of your thought the remembrance of bodily deeds done previously, or thoughts of other people's deeds. (This is not much of a thing to master when you possess a mature spirit of devotion, but you are obliged to do as I say when you have no such devotion; and I know it is then much harder to accomplish.) And set your intent and purpose upon your Lord Jesus, as if you would not seek, experience, or find anything but the grace, spiritual presence, teaching, and comfort of the Lord Jesus Christ.

At first you will
see only your own
spiritual ugliness.
This is hard going, for vain thoughts are bound to pass thickly into your heart in an effort to drag your thought down to their level. But you can withstand this distraction through the stable mind of Jesus, and if you do this you shall already find something of what you are looking for, if not yet fully the Jesus whom you are seeking. What will that be? Truly, nothing at first but the dark and painful image of your own soul, which has neither the light of knowing nor consciousness of love or affection. This image, if you regard it imaginatively, is all draped over with black, stinking garments of sin—pride, envy, wrath, sloth, covetousness, gluttony, and lechery: it is the figure of your unregenerate will. [19]

Surely this is not the image of Jesus. It is an image of sin; as St. Paul calls it, a body of sin and death. This unreformed image and black shadow you are bearing about with you wherever you go, and out from it seeps a mist of sins, great and small. Just as out of the true image (when it is reformed in beams of spiritual light) shine ardent desires, pure affections, wise thoughts, and all honest virtues ascending up into heaven; so also out of this dark image seeps a poisonous mist of pride, envy, and the like.

And all of these things deform in you the potential integrity of man, reducing it to the likeness of a beast.

Perhaps you are beginning to wonder what this unreformed image actually resembles. So that you do not ponder overlong, I will tell you that it resembles no physical thing. What is it then? Truly it is nothing, no thing— as you may well discover if you put to the test what I have said to you.[20]

This darkened image is a spiritual "nothingness."

In this condition, if you draw into yourself and turn your thought inward from all physical things, then you shall find nothing at all in which the soul may rest. This nothingness is a kind of darkness of consciousness, a deprivation of love and light, just as sin is nothing but a lack of God.

If in fact your condition was such that the ground of sin was thoroughly broken up and dried out in you, and your soul was rightly reformed to the image of Jesus, then when you drew into yourself in your heart you would not find that vacuum, but rather discover Jesus. And I do not mean that you would discover only the mere memory of his name either, but that you would find Jesus Christ himself in your conscience,[21] readily teaching you. What you would be finding then is his light of understanding, with no murkiness of ignorance; you would be finding love and pleasure in him, with no pain of bitterness and backbiting.

But since you are not yet reformed, when your soul turns inward, withdrawing from all physical concerns, and finds there nothing but darkness and the burden of sin, it can seem like a hundred winters before it is able to escape by means of some physical distraction of insignificant thought. And small wonder, for anyone who came home to his house and found nothing inside but stinking smoke and a chiding wife would soon run out of it again. Even so, when your soul finds no comfort in itself, but a black, reeking smoke of spiritual blindness and excessive chiding of carnal thought crying out upon you, so that you may have no peace, it soon becomes so irritated that it gets itself outside again somehow. This is the clouding of conscience I have been speaking of, when it is confronted by the darkening of your natural image.

Temptation to rationalize and beg the question

Now you may well find it hard to think of this un-reformed natural image as a vacuum, a nothingness, or non-being. Its very evil seems to constitute something, after all—self-love, for one thing. And in any case you may be wondering how it is fair to say that such a dark image could reside in you. Here you are, having forsaken the world and entered into a religious house where you have dealings with no one and are not contending with anyone. I can almost hear you saying, "I do not make a fuss, I neither buy nor sell, have no worldly business, but by the mercy of God keep myself chaste and free of worldly indulgence. In keeping myself to this purpose I pray, rouse myself up, and work physically and spiritually as much as I can. How then can this negative image be so strong in me as you suggest?"

In the garden of your soul

To this I answer that I believe that you do all these works and more, and yet what I am saying may still be true. You are busy, energetically endeavoring to stop up seepages of sin into the garden of your heart, but perhaps overlooking the very wellspring of the problem. In this you could be like a man who had in his garden a polluted well with many irrigation ditches running from it. He went and dammed up the ditches, but left the wellspring itself intact, imagining that his problem was solved. But the water then sprung up at the well-head into a stagnant, underground pool which gradually grew and grew until it had inundated and corrupted all the garden, despite that no foul water ever appeared again on the surface.

Repression of sur-face impurities is no solution.

It can be the same way for you and me, even if we have had the grace and strength to stop up our external ditches, failing to beware properly the source within. Truly, unless you stop and cleanse that as much as you are able, it will corrupt all the flowers in the garden of your soul, no matter how beautiful they have seemed to human eyes.

But now you may be saying, "How shall I know that I

have been successful in stopping up the source of this pollution even if I work hard at it?" And to this question I shall offer you a test, a measurement by which you shall know how much it has been brought under control, or how little.

VI

THE MEASURE OF LOVE

A good man for the love of God will fast, work, go on pilgrimage, or forsake the pleasures of the world all in sincerity and integrity of heart without pretense. He shall have his reward in the bliss of heaven. A hypocrite for vainglory and self-promotion will do the same deeds and receive his reward here (Matthew 6:5).

The value of spiritual endeavor is determined by motives of the heart.

Likewise, a true preacher of God's word, rich in charitable love and in meekness, called of God and received by his holy Church, shall have a special reward, a crown for his preaching. And hypocrites and charlatans, who have neither meekness nor charity and are sent neither by God nor his holy Church, when they preach they have their reward here.

A good layman, for the love of God, may help to build churches, chapels, abbeys, hospitals, and perform other works of mercy. He shall have have his reward in the bliss of heaven—not for the deeds themselves, but for the good will and charitable love that he had as a gift of God and then exercised to do his good work. Another such person for vanity of himself, praise of the world, and advancement of his own name does the same good deeds, and he has his reward here.

The distinction in all of these cases is that the one person has charity and the other has none. Which person is in the one situation, and which is in the other, the Lord himself knows. And none but he knows.

CHARITY AND APPEARANCES

Therefore, we should love and honor all persons in our hearts, and approve and receive all their deeds that have the appearance of goodness, even though it is possible that some of the doers may in God's sight be badly motivated. This does not apply, of course, in the case of those who are openly heretical or evil. These types we should flee, eschewing their presence or association with them, and we should reprove their deeds as long as they remain rebels against God and his holy Church.

If someone who is a kind of living curse builds a church or feeds a poor man, you may appropriately deem it as nothing, for spiritually speaking, so it is. And if an open heretic and charlatan, rebel to the Church, should preach and teach—even if he converts a hundred thousand souls—you may believe that the deeds do him no spiritual good. For such men are plainly out of charity, without which anything we may do is nothing.

The validating motive is love. Accordingly, I say it is a great victory for a person just to be able to love his fellow Christian in charity. All this is plainly proclaimed by St. Paul, who in praising charity says: "Though I speak with the tongues of men and of angels, and have not charity, I am become as sounding brass or a tinkling cymbal. And though I have the gift of prophecy, and understand all mysteries, and all knowledge; and though I have all faith, so that I could remove mountains, and have not charity, it profits me nothing. And though I bestow all my goods to feed the poor, and though I give my body to be burned, and have not charity, it profiteth me nothing" (1 Corinthians 13:1-3). Here it seems by St. Paul's word that one may do all sorts of practical deeds without possessing charity. And yet we know that charity is nothing else but to love God and our neighbor as ourselves (Matthew 22:37-39).

CHARITY AND JUDGMENT

How then can any miserable wretch here on earth, whatever his status or position, have delight or trust or confidence in himself or anything that he can do (or thinks he can do) in his own strength and natural reason? For all of it, if it is without love and charity toward his fellow Christian, is worth nothing. And this charity may not be had by some self-generated effort, for as St. Paul tells us, it is a gift of God granted to meek souls.

Who then dares boldly to say: "I have charity" or "I am in charity"? Truly, none of us can say this with confidence except one who is perfectly and unfeignedly meek. Others may believe themselves to be so, or hope that they are in charity by exhibiting signs of charity. But he that is perfectly meek experiences it, and therefore is alone able to say it truthfully.

Only the meek truly dwell in love.

This was the kind of meekness possessed by Paul when he said: "Who shall separate us from the love of Christ? Shall tribulation, or distress, or persecution, or famine, or nakedness, or peril, or sword?" (Romans 8:35). And he answered himself and said that nothing shall be able to separate us from the love of God which is in Jesus Christ our Lord (verse 39).

Many people do deeds of charity and have no actual love, as I have been saying. For to reprove a sinner for his sin with the purpose of his amending while there is yet time, that is a deed of charity. But to hate the sinner instead of the sin, that is against charitable love. One who is himself truly meek can distinguish one from the other, and nobody else can. One could, in fact, have all the intelligence of the philosophers and not manage this distinction. He might be able to hate the sin in other persons inasmuch as he hated it in himself, but he could not love the individual sinner in charitable love for all his philosophy. Even a man who has clerical training and education in divinity and yet is not genuinely meek will err and stumble here, confusing the one with the other. And meekness, worthy as it is and to be received as a gift from

God, may not be learned from the knowledge of men.

Now, I suppose it is possible that you are beginning to be uneasy when I say to you that charitable love cannot be obtained by any effort on your own part. What then should you do? And in reply to this I say to you that there is nothing so hard to come by through dint of your own effort as charitable love; and also the contrary, that there is no gift of God which may be had so easily as this love. Our Lord gives no gift so gladly or commonly as he does charity.

"How then shall I obtain it?" you ask. Be meek and lowly in spirit, and you shall have it. And what involves less effort than to be meek? Truly nothing. So it seems that there ought to be nothing so easily come by as charitable love, and accordingly you ought not to be intimidated. Just be meek and have it.

Listen to what St. James the apostle says: "God resisteth the proud but giveth grace unto the humble" (James 4:6). And this grace is properly known in charity, for according to the measure of your meekness or humility shall you have charitable love.

"Imperfect" love suffices for salvation. If you have meekness imperfectly—that is, only by your own willpower, and not in your affection—then you shall have imperfect charity. This is still a good thing, sufficing for salvation. As David said: "Thine eyes did see my substance, yet being imperfect" (Psalm 139:16). But if you have perfect meekness you shall have perfect love, and that is clearly best. The first we need to have if we wish to be saved; the second we ought to seek after.

Now, if you ask me how one is to be perfectly meek, you shall obtain from me no further answer at this time but this: he is truly meek who truthfully knows and is conscious of himself as he actually is.

TRUTH IN THE INWARD PARTS

Now let us consider again this business of the negative image. It is necessary to discover how much bitterness and envy (of which you are not aware) is hidden in the depths of your heart.

Look carefully and consider yourself wisely when stirrings of bitterness and envy against your fellow Christian are welling up in your heart. The more stirred up you are by feelings of self-pity, bitterness, or wicked will against some other person, the more dominant will this negative image loom in your soul. The more you grouch in impatience either against God (for tribulation, sickness, or other physical impediments sent to you by him) or against your fellow Christian (for anything he has done against you), the less is the image of Jesus reformed in you.

I do not mean to say that every grumble or irritation is a deadly sin. But I do say that each is an impediment to purity of heart and peace of conscience, and keeps you from a full experience of charitable love such as you need if you are to come to a life which is truly contemplative, that is, which really looks upon Jesus.

To that end, I say that you ought to be cleansing your heart not only from deadly sins but from venial ones too, as much as is possible to you, and praying that the very source of sin might by the grace of Jesus Christ be somewhat tempered in you. For even if you feel no evil will against any fellow Christian for a time, yet you may not be confident that the well of bitterness in your heart is really stopped up, nor are you yet a master of the virtue of charitable love. For as soon as someone touches you a little by an angry or shrewd word, you will have occasion to test whether your heart has yet been made whole in a fullness of charity. And the more you are stirred up and ill-willed against another person, the further you are from perfect love of your fellow Christians. The less you are stirred up in this way, the nearer you will be to charity.

Do not shrink from testing yourself for charity.

THE STANDARD OF LOVE

These are the tokens by which you will know if you love your fellow Christian, and what example you ought to take from Christ in learning to love him.

What it really comes to is this: if you are not stirred up against such a person in anger while faking an outward cheer, and have no secret hatred in your heart, despising him or judging him or considering him worthless; if the more shame and villainy he does to you in word or deed, the more pity and compassion you show toward him, almost as you would for someone who was emotionally or mentally distressed; and if you are so compelled by love that you actually cannot find it in your heart to hate him, but instead you pray for him, help him out, and desire his amending (not only with your mouth, as hypocrites do, but with a true feeling of love in your heart): *then* you will be in perfect charity toward your fellow Christian.

The example of Stephen

This sort of charitable love was exhibited perfectly by St. Stephen, when he prayed for those who stoned him to death. This is the love Christ counseled to all who would be his perfect followers when he said: "Love your enemies: do good to them that hate you, pray for them which despitefully use you" (Luke 6:28; Matthew 5:44). And therefore if you would follow Christ, be like him in this way. Learn to love your enemies and sinful men, for all of them may be your fellow Christians.

The example of Jesus with Judas

Stop and think how Christ loved Judas, who was both his mortal enemy and a sinful dog. How good Christ was to him, how benign, how courteous, how humble toward him whom he knew to be damnable. He chose him for his apostle and sent him to preach with the other apostles. He gave him power to work miracles. He showed to him the same good cheer in word and deed. He shared with him his precious Body, and preached to him in the same manner as he did to the other apostles. He did not condemn him openly; nor did he abuse him or despise him, nor ever speak evil of him (and yet even if he had done all of that, it would simply have been to tell the truth!). And above all, when Judas seized him, he kissed him and called him his friend.

All this charitable love Christ showed to Judas whom

he knew to be damnable—without feigning or flattering, but in truthfulness of good love and pure charity. For though it might seem to us that Judas was unworthy to have any gift of God, or any token of love because of his wickedness, nevertheless in God's eyes it was worthy and reasonable that our Lord should show himself to him as he is.

For he is love and goodness, and therefore it is charac- teristic of him to show love and goodness to all his crea- tures, as he did to Judas. Follow after him somewhat if you can, for even though you are imprisoned within the walls of your bodily dwelling, nevertheless in your heart, where the place of love is, you may be enabled to have part of such a love toward your fellow Christians. Whoever imag- ines himself to be a perfect follower of Jesus Christ's teach- ing and life—as some persons judge themselves to be, in- asmuch as they teach and preach and are poor in worldly goods, as Christ was—and still cannot follow Christ in love and charity, loving his fellow Christians every one, good and ill, friends and foes, without pretense, flattery, despising them in his heart, or indulging himself in re- sentment or self-serving reproof, well, truly that person deceives himself. In fact, the nearer to Christ he imagines himself to be in such a state, the further away in fact he is. For Christ said to those who would be his followers: "This is my commandment, that you love mutually as I have loved you" (John 13:34). Or we may also translate it: "This is my bidding, that you love *together* as I love you, for if you love as I have loved you, then are you my dis- ciples."

Try to follow this model.

Now you may be asking: "How is it that we should love someone who is bad as well as someone who is good?" And my reply is that you should, in charity, love both those who are bad and those who are good—but not for the same reason.

For example, let us consider how it is that you should love your fellow Christian as you do yourself. First, you ought to love yourself only in God, or else for the sake of

Proper love for the self

God. You are loving yourself in God when your life is rightly ordered in grace and virtues. You are not loving your own self, but that righteousness and virtue which God gives you. You are loving yourself in God, for actually you are not loving your own self but rather God. Moreover, you are to love yourself for God's sake, and inasmuch as you are in deadly sin and want to be made righteous and virtuous before him, you are not loving yourself as you are (which is unrighteous), but actually as you would be.

Proper love for one's neighbor   Just so should you love your fellow Christians. If they are good and right-living, you should love them by charitable love in God, for that goodness and righteousness of him that they bear. Then you are loving God in them, expressed in their goodness and right living.

This is of course much easier than if they are bad and in deadly sin, offering much evidence that they are not in grace. Yet even in such a case you should love them—not as they are, or pretending that they are good and right living when they are not, but you should love them for God's sake, as he loves them, yearning that they may become good and live rightly. And so you should hate in such persons only that which is contrary to righteousness, that is, sin. This is, as I understand it, also the teaching of St. Augustine.[22]

He that is truly meek, or would be meek, can love his fellow Christians. And nobody else can do so.

CONFORMING TO THE IMAGE OF JESUS

Whoever hopes to come to the exercise and full experience of contemplation and comes not by the way I have been speaking about— that is, by way of steadfast focus on the precious example of the life of Jesus Christ and his Passion, and by participating in his virtues—he comes not by the door, and therefore as a thief he shall be cast out.

I am not saying that it is impossible for certain persons to have a kind of glimmering of what contemplative faith

is all about; by God's gift some persons are given an inkling of this quite early in their Christian life. But a steadfast consciousness focused on him cannot be had in a
flash. For Christ is both the door and the doorkeeper, and
without his life and vestments may no one come in. As he
says himself: "No man cometh to the Father but by me"
(John 14:6). That is also to say that no one may come to
a contemplative focus on the Godhead except he first be
reformed in a fullness of meekness and charity to the likeness or image of Jesus in his pattern of human life.

ENVOY

Well, now I have told you a little of what I think, first
of the definition of contemplation, and then of the ways
by which grace may lead us to it. Not that I claim to possess in consciousness and experience all I have been describing. Nevertheless, I would by these words, such as
they are, first to stir up my own negligence to do better
than I have been doing. And my purpose is also to stir you
and any other man or woman choosing the state of contemplative life to work more diligently and meekly to live
up to that calling by such simple words as God has given
me grace to speak.

Accordingly, if you find any words here which move
you or comfort you in the love of God, thank him, for it is
his gift and not a matter of words. And if this book does
not comfort you, or you are not able to take it in too readily, do not study it overlong. Rather, put it aside until
another time, and give yourself over to prayer or other
worthy occupation. Take it as it will come, and not all at
once.

Finally, do not take these words of mine too strictly. In
cases when you are led to think on good advice that I have
spoken too cryptically, either because of lack of English
or a deficiency of my intellect, I plead with you to amend

my text— though only as necessary. And remember: much of what I have written to you is not intended for persons of active life, lay people, but only pertains to you and to others who have the vocation of contemplative life.

The grace of our Lord Jesus Christ be with you. Amen.

Book II
THE PROGRESS OF THE SOUL

I

THE IMAGE OF GOD

I nasmuch as you have greatly desired it and asked that out of charity you might hear more concerning that image which I have partly described to you already, I will gladly respect your wishes. Let me then attempt, as I am upheld in the grace of our Lord Jesus Christ in whom I trust utterly, to expound a little more on the character of this image.

In the first instance, if you wish to know in plain language what I mean by this "image," let me say straightaway that I understand nothing else by this term except the soul. Your soul, my soul, any person's rational soul, is an image. And it is a most worthy image, for it is the image of God. As the apostle says, man is "the image and glory of God" (1 Corinthians 11:7).

That is, man is in the image of God, and made according to the image and likeness of him—not in outward physical appearance, but in the faculties of inner being. As Holy Writ says: "God created man in his own image" (Genesis 1:27); that is, our Lord God shaped mankind in soul to his own image and likeness. And this is precisely the image of which I have been speaking. This image, fashioned according to the image of God in its first making, was wonderfully fair and bright, full of burning love and spiritual light.

Mankind is made in the image of God.

Disfigurement

But as we have seen, through the sin of the first man, Adam, this image was disfigured and misshapen into another likeness, falling from spiritual life and heavenly sustenance into the painful muddiness and lust of our present life. Exiled from the heritage of heaven that it was intended to have, it toppled into the wretchedness of the world and after to the prison of hell, where it had condemned itself eternally. From this prison to its heavenly heritage no return would be possible unless the image could somehow be reformed to its original shape and created likeness.

But such a reformation could not be achieved by any mortal man. It required being done by him who is more than a man, God himself. It was rationally necessary that if mankind was to be saved, he would have to reform and restore us to that bliss which, in his eternal generosity, he had created for us in the beginning.

How then our fallen image is able to be reformed, and how it is reformed to that first likeness by the one who first gave it its form, is the subject and intent of this writing, as God shall enable me by his grace.

RESTORATION OF THE IMAGE

You may ask how it should be true that the image of God which is in man's soul might be restored here in this life to approach his likeness. Surely it seems that no, this is impossible. For anyone in whom the image was truly reformed would possess a stable mind, clarified vision, and a pure, burning love for God and spiritual things in an everlasting and unbroken manner, even as it was in the beginning. And those qualities are in no creature, as you know, which lives here this present life.

All of our faculties are damaged by sin.

Concerning yourself, for example, you can well enough say that you consider yourself to be far from the standard. Your memory, your intellect, and the love which is in your soul are so much set upon earthly things that you are all too little conscious of spiritual things. You are experiencing no reforming in your self, but are so compassed about with the black image of sinfulness (despite every effort to control it), that on whatever side you look you feel yourself to be befouled and stained with the carnality of this dark negative image.

And perhaps you are not experiencing any other sort of transformation of carnal to spiritual character either; neither in the private depths of your soul nor in your outward behavior. It is understandable, then, that you should come to the conclusion that this original image might never be reformed in you. Or at least if you accept that it can be reformed, then you are curious as to how it can really happen. To these uncertainties let me offer the following answers.

There are two degrees of reformation of the image of God which is man's soul. One of these is in fullness, the other partial. A completeness of reformation may not be had by us in this life, but it is delayed until after this life in the bliss of heaven; there the soul shall be fully reformed. And it will then be reformed utterly—not merely to that estate it had in creation, or might have had yet through grace without the fall—but by the great mercy and boundless generosity of God it shall be restored to much greater bliss and higher joy than it might have had even if it had never fallen. For then shall the soul receive the whole infilling of God in all its faculties, without the distraction of any other affections; and it shall see mankind as God intended, in the person of Jesus, above the nature of angels and united to the Godhead. For then shall Jesus, both God and man, be all in all, and only he and no other but himself. As the prophet said: "The LORD alone shall be exalted on that day" (Isaiah 2:11).

The body of man shall also then be glorified, for it shall receive in full a rich dowry of immortality with all the accompanying benefits. This will be the soul's portion with the body—and indeed much more than I can say—but all in the bliss of heaven, and not in this mortal life. For although our Lord died on the cross to provide for this complete restoration of human souls, nevertheless it was

Full reformation can only be had in heaven.

not his will to grant complete restoration instantly after his Passion to all chosen souls living at that time. Rather, he delayed its completion until the Last Day, and that for a reason.

It is true that our Lord Jesus in his mercy has ordained a certain number of souls to salvation. This number was not yet fulfilled at the time of his Passion, and required that there should be a passage of time through natural generations of men and women until the number should be completed. If it had been that after the cross, every soul that believed in him should have been blessed absolutely and fully reformed without any further abiding here, it seems likely that there would have been no one then alive who would have failed to receive the faith, in order to have this manifest blessing. And then, of course, all generation would have ceased. Accordingly, we who are now alive, his chosen souls, and other souls who come after us, could not have been born, and our Lord would have failed of his number. But that is clearly impossible![23]

And so our Lord provided much better for us, in that he delayed the full reforming of man's soul until that Last Day. As St. Paul says: "God [has] provided some better thing for us, that they without us should not be made perfect" (Hebrews 11:40). That is, our Lord provided better for us by delaying the completion of his reforming than if he had granted it all at once then, and for this reason: that the chosen souls of these who have gone before may not come to a complete rest without us who come after them. Another reason is this: man in his first creation by God was provided with free will and made able to choose whether he would have God fully or not at all. Since mankind would not choose God at that time, but miserably fell away from him, it follows that if he is afterward to be reformed, he should be set again in the same state of free will that was his in the beginning, and made to decide whether he would receive the benefit of his recreation or not. And so this may be part of the reason the soul of man was not fully reformed immediately following the Passion of our Lord Jesus Christ.

The other degree of reformation is partial, and this kind of reformation of the soul may be had in our present life. Indeed, unless it is experienced in this life it cannot be had at all, nor can the soul ever be saved. But this reformation is itself of two kinds. One is in faith only; the other is in faith and experience. The first, reformation by faith alone, is sufficient for salvation. The second is worthy to increase our reward in heaven. The first may be had easily and in short order, the second not so, but only through long experience and spiritual growth. The first may be born simply of the conviction of sin—for though a person feels nothing in himself but the depredations of sin, he may, if he resists that sin, be reformed in faith toward the likeness of God. But the second kind of reformation quiets the urgency of our carnal appetite and worldly desires, and suffers no such blemishes to abide unresisted in the soul's image.

But a partial reformation is possible here and is of two kinds:

The first kind of reformation is then only the setting out and early growth of the soul. This is the experience of many lay people. But the second is for souls that are being perfected, and for those who want to be contemplative. In the first reforming, the image of sin is not yet destroyed, but continues to linger in the consciousness. But the second reforming is a process whereby the old feelings of this negative image of sin are burned away, bringing into the soul a new and gracious spiritual consciousness through the work of the Holy Spirit. The first is good, the second is better. But that other degree, that comes only in the bliss of heaven, that is altogether best.

Reformation in faith;

in spiritual experience

II

THE SPIRITUAL PILGRIM

You say that you covet some means of endeavor by which you might come more nearly to the kind of soul's reformation of which I have been speaking. Well, I shall try to tell you something further of what I have been thinking, and by the grace of our Lord Jesus present the shortest and readiest help I know to this end. And how it may come about I shall tell you by the example of a good pilgrim, as follows.

There was once a man who wanted to go to Jerusalem. Because he did not know the way himself, he went to another man he expected would know the way, and asked how he should proceed to come to that city. The other man said to him that he could not hope to get there without great difficulties and much travail, because the way was long and imperiled by hordes of thieves and robbers, as well as many other hindrances such as can beset a traveler. And there was a great diversity of routes, so it seemed, leading there, along which people were killed and despoiled every day, and prevented from coming to their coveted destination. Nevertheless, one sure way existed. Whoever would take that road and keep to it, the man guaranteed that he would come to the city of Jerusalem, and never lose his life through murder or peril along the way. True, it was likely that he would be robbed

Parable of a pilgrim

and beaten a number of times, and suffer much distress in the going, but he would keep his life safe.

Keep your desti-
nation ever in
your mind.

The pilgrim then said: "If I can really preserve my life safely so as to come to the place I covet, I do not care what mischief I have to suffer en route. Therefore say to me what you will, and truly I will endeavor to do as you say." The other man answered him and said: "Lo, I set you upon the right way. This is the way, that you keep the counsel that I am about to offer you. Whatever you hear or see or experience that threatens to block your way, do not linger with it of your own will, or tarry at rest hoping it will go away. Do not consider it, take any pleasure in it, or fear it. Rather, press ever onward in your journey, and remember that you want to be in Jerusalem. For that is what you desire, and nothing else but that.

"If someone robs and vandalizes you, beats you, scorns you, or despises you, do not struggle against these things if you want to keep your life. Rather, compose yourself, come to terms with the harm you have endured, and go forth as if nothing had happened, so that you suffer no additional hurt. And also, if people want to delay you with tales and feed you with falsehoods, attempting to draw you into mirth and so cause you to abandon your pilgrimage, turn to them a deaf ear, and answer not again. Say nothing else except that you want to be in Jerusalem. And if people offer you gifts and strive to make you rich with worldly goods, pay no attention to them. Think always on Jerusalem. And if you will keep to this way and do as I have said, I guarantee your life, that you shall not be slain but come to the place of your desire."

Jerusalem: the
vision of peace

Now to our spiritual purpose. "Jerusalem" is as much as to say "the vision of peace,"[24] and signifies contemplation in perfect love of God. For contemplation is nothing else but a vision of Jesus, in whom alone is true peace. Accordingly, if you really desire to come to this blessed vision of true peace and be a true pilgrim toward Jerusalem, I shall, even though I have never been there, nevertheless set you on the path toward it as best I can.

The beginning of the highway on which you should travel is reformation in faith, grounded meekly in the faith and ordinance of Holy Church, as I have said before. For you may trust securely that even though you have sinned in the past, if you are reformed by the sacrament of repentance after the ordinance of Holy Church, then you are on the right path.

Now then, since you have begun in the right route, if you want to speed your passage and make a good journey of it, you will need to have two things often in your mind: meekness and love. That is, you will be able to say: "I am nothing, I have nothing, I covet nothing—but One." You ought to have the meaning of these words in your intention and soul's habit always (even though you have not always these words themselves formed in your thought, for that is not important).

Meekness says: "I am nothing and I have nothing." Love says: "I desire only one thing, and that is Jesus." These two strings, well fastened in remembrance of Jesus, make good harmony in the harp of your soul when they are artfully touched with the fingers of the intellect. The lower you strike upon the one, the higher will the other sound.

Travel in meekness and in love.

The less you feel you are or have in your own strength, by virtue of meekness, the more you will covet Jesus in the desire of love. I am speaking here not only of that meekness which a soul experiences in view of its own sin, frailties, or wretchedness in this present life, or in comparing itself to the worthiness of fellow Christians, because even though this meekness is true and healthful, it is nevertheless rough and carnal in its outworking, not pure or gentle or lovely. I mean also that meekness which a soul experiences through grace in a vision and beholding of the boundless humanity and wonderful goodness of Jesus. If you cannot yet see this with your spiritual eyes, I hope that you will believe it. For through a vision of his humanity either entirely by faith or in spiritual experience you will come to regard yourself not only as the most

Measure yourself not against other believers but against Jesus himself.

miserable of sinners but also as nothing in the substance of your soul, regardless of how much or how little you have sinned.

And this is lovely meekness. For by comparison with Jesus, who is all, you are in truth nothing. Consider too that you have nothing, but are like a vessel standing empty, containing nothing in yourself. For however many deeds you do in your outward life, or inner life, until you have and experience the love of Jesus you do not have anything. With that precious liqueur only may your soul be really filled, and with no other. And inasmuch as that alone is so precious and worthy, whatever you have or do ought to be counted as worthless without a vision of the love of Jesus. Cast everything else behind you and forget it, so that you can have that which is best of all

Becoming poor in spirit

Just as an actual pilgrim traveling to Jerusalem leaves behind him his house and land, wife and child, making himself poor and empty of all he has possessed that he might more readily travel without hindrances, just so for you if you want to be a spiritual pilgrim. You ought to strip yourself naked of all that you have, both good deeds and bad, and cast them all behind you. Be so poor in your own spirit that there will be nothing left on which you are leaning or taking rest, and be always desiring more grace and love and always seeking the spiritual presence of Jesus.

If you do this, then you will be committing your heart wholly and without reserve toward Jerusalem, longing to be there and no place else. This is to say that you will be setting your heart entirely and without reserve to have nothing but the love of Jesus and such spiritual vision of him as he will bestow, for to that end only were you created and redeemed: he is your beginning and end, your joy and your bliss.

Therefore, whatever else you have, be you ever so rich in other spiritual and bodily deeds, unless you have that, and are conscious of having it, consider yourself as having nothing. Imprint this reasoning on the intentions of your heart, and soberly cleave to it. It will save you from all kinds of peril on your voyage, so that you shall never perish. And it will protect you from thieves and robbers (which I think of as unclean spirits), that though they despoil and beat you through various temptations, still your spiritual life shall be kept safe. And so, to put it concisely, if you keep to the route I advise, you shall escape at last all perils and mischiefs and come to the city of Jerusalem almost before you know it.

Now then: you are on the road, and you know the name of the place to which you are traveling. Begin then to set out on your journey. Your traveling forth is, of course, nothing else but spiritual labor—and physical labor too, as need arises. You shall proceed in discretion and in this fashion: whatever work you are called to do, according to the degree or state of life in which you are placed, and whether materially or spiritually, do what best helps you in this gracious desire you have to love Jesus. Whatever makes this love more whole, open, and powerful in virtue and goodness, then that is the work I hold to be best. Whether it is preaching, thinking, reading, or working, whatever most strengthens your heart and will in the love of Jesus, and most successfully draws your thought and affection away from worldly vanity, it is good for you to be doing that.

Progress toward Jerusalem is growth in desire for Jesus.

If it happens that through much endeavor the good of any of these seems to lessen, so that you wonder if another might not be more profitable, and you are experiencing more grace in another, then take it up and get to work on it and leave the first for a season. For while your desire and the yearning of your heart toward Jesus should be fixed and unchanging, your spiritual endeavors that support you in prayer and in thought, feeding, and nourishing your desire may be diverse and usefully interchanged as you are led by grace in the application to them of your own heart.

It occurs with spiritual exercises and desire much as it does with sticks of wood and a fire. The more sticks you lay on the fire, the bigger is the fire. Just so, the more avenues of spiritual endeavor a person has in his thought to sustain his desire, the mightier and more brightly burning shall be his desire toward God. Therefore look wisely to the work you can do best, since that most aids you in sustaining a fullness of desire toward Jesus. If you are free to do it, and not restricted by your religious rule, then do it. But do not bind yourself to any spiritual exercise so rigidly that you are prevented from a freedom of heart in loving Jesus if grace for that should come to you in some special way.

There are many ways open to you by which to nourish this desire.

Let me tell you what spiritual exercises are always good and necessary to be kept. It is always good to pursue any exercise that encourages the acquisition of virtue and discourages sin. Such an exercise ought never to be abandoned, for you will always be meek, patient, sober, and chaste if you persevere well in it; and the other virtues will also follow. But you should prepare to leave off any spiritual exercise which bids to prevent your access to something more spiritually fruitful when the opportunity for that has presented itself clearly. So if someone has the usual practice of saying many prayers of the rosary[25] or thinking according to some pattern of meditative thought for long stretches or waking or kneeling for long periods or using any other bodily aid to devotion, he or she ought to leave off this practice when reasonable cause presents itself, or if more grace seems to be coming by another means.

III
TRUE AND FALSE LIGHT

There is a kind of darkness and night of the soul which is good and even restful, though of short duration on our way. It consists in desire and longing for the love of Jesus while we are still in a state of "blind" thinking about him, when we are for a time unable to "see" him clearly.[26] Afterwards, how good then and how blessed it is to feel his love and to be illumined with his blessed invisible light so as to see truthfulness, which light a soul receives when the night passes and dayspring comes. The dark night of the soul is what I imagine the prophet to have been talking about when he said: "With my soul have I desired thee in the night: yea, with my spirit within me will I seek thee early" (Isaiah 26:9).

TRUSTING GOD IN THE DARKNESS

It is much better to be hidden in this kind of dark night from a beholding of the world, even though the experience is painful, than to be out and involved in the false pleasures that seem so shining and comfortable to those who are blind to spiritual light. For when you are in the darkness of spiritual doubt you are much nearer Jerusalem than when you are in the midst of false light.

Times of spiritual
struggle can be
occasions for faith
and love.

Therefore you should give over your heart completely to the stirrings of grace, accustoming yourself to dwell now and then in this darkness, often testing yourself to see if you are at home there. It shall soon enough be made restful to you, and the true light of spiritual knowledge shall then rise upon you—if not at once, then little by little. As the prophet says: "The people that walked in darkness have seen a great light" (Isaiah 9:2). To those dwelling in the shadow of death, light has dawned. The light of grace has arisen, and shall still arise upon those who are called to walk through the valley of the shadow of death, in that darkness of the soul that is like unto death.

Death slays a living body and all its physical consciousness of that which is. But the desire to love Jesus experienced in darkness slays sinfulness, carnal affections, and unclean thoughts, and draws you close to Jerusalem. You are not quite there yet, but by sudden glimmerings that shine out through small windows in that city you shall grow able to see it from afar, long before you get there.

Be well aware that even when your soul learns to accept the darkness of this present life restfully, without being troubled by worldly vanities, it is not yet where it should be. It is not yet clothed in light, nor transformed by the fire of love. But it senses that there is something higher that it does not yet know or possess, and longs to have it, ardently yearning after it. And this "something higher" is nothing other than that celestial Jerusalem, which is like the city which the prophet Ezekiel saw in his visions (Ezekiel 40-42).

The City set on a
hill

He said that he saw a city set upon a hill, sloping to the south, and that to his sight it was, when it was measured, no more in length and breadth than a rood—that is, six cubits and a palm in length. Yet as soon as he was brought into the city and looked about him, then he thought that it was amazingly large, for he saw many halls and chambers, both public and private; he saw gates and porches, inner and outer courts, and many more buildings than I can enumerate, in length and breadth altogether many hundreds of cubits. All this was a wonder to him, that the city within was so long and spacious that had seemed so little in his sight when he was yet outside it.

This City signifies for us the perfect love of God, set upon the hill of contemplation. He sees well who recognizes that there is such a thing, and that it lies a little beyond the desert of human endeavor, though he does not yet see what lies within. But if he is enabled to come to the hill of contemplation, then he sees much more than he saw at first.

COUNTERFEIT LIGHT

But beware, now, of the Noonday Demon[27] that counterfeits light as if it is straight from Jerusalem, but it is nothing of the kind. For the fiend sees that our Lord Jesus reveals light to his lovers of truth; therefore, in order to deceive those who are unwise, he makes a show of light. It always proves false under color of the true light, and yet still he beguiles some. I therefore want to say something about how it is a soul may recognize the light of truth when it shines from God, and distinguish it from that artificial light of the Enemy.

The devil's deceits

Let me offer a simple example from astronomy. Sometimes the firmament shows a kind of light which seems to be the sun itself, but is not; and of course, sometimes the true sun is revealed truly. Discerning one from the other consists in this: the artificial sun does not show itself except between two black, rainy clouds. Because the sun is nearby, there shines out from the clouds a light which appears to be the sun but is not. The sun itself is revealed when the firmament is clear or at least substantially clear of such black clouds.

Now to our purpose: some people seem as though they forsake the love of the world and intend to come to the love of God and the light of understanding in him, but they will not come out from the midst of this murkiness of soul that I have spoken of before. They will not recognize themselves for what they have been before, and are still

Spiritual opportunists

through sin, nor acknowledge how they remain in their own strength nothing before God. They are not diligent to enter into themselves, forsaking outward concerns so as to slay the wicked turmoil of sinfulness in their hearts—pride, envy, wrath, and other sins—through a consistent desire toward Jesus in prayer, in thoughtful meditation, silence, and repentance, as devout and holy men and women have always done. Rather, as soon as they have begun to forsake the world with respect to external appearances, or very soon afterward, they imagine themselves to be holy and in possession of a spiritual understanding of the gospel and Holy Writ.

Notably, if they keep the letter of the commandments of God and keep themselves from bodily sin, they imagine that they love God perfectly. And they therefore immediately set out to preach and teach all others, as if they had received the grace of understanding and perfection of charitable love through a unique personal gift of the Holy Spirit. And they tend to be much more stirred up about such things than others, supposing themselves possessed of great insight, which they feel is given to them suddenly without study beforehand, and also a great fervor of love, so it seems, to preach truth and righteousness to their fellow Christians. Therefore they count it a grace of God that he visits them with his blessed light in preference to other souls.

Nevertheless, if such folk really look about themselves, they will see that this light of insight and heat of passion that they feel comes not from the true sun, the Lord Jesus; rather, it comes from the Noonday Demon that feigns light and likens himself to the sun.

Recognizing imposters   This is the way that such counterfeiters shall be recognized. The light of knowledge of insight which is feigned by the fiend to a murky soul is always revealed between two black and stormy clouds. The over-cloud is presumption, the nether-cloud is the down-putting and undercutting of one's fellow Christians. Now whatever light of knowledge or experience of fervor shines upon a soul, when it is accompanied by presumption, self-promotion, and disdain of one's fellow Christians at the same time, it is not a light of grace granted by the Holy Spirit. This is so even when the knowledge in itself is of the truth. No, it is either of the devil if it comes suddenly, or of man's own wit if it comes by study. And it ought to be more widely recognized that this kind of feigned light is not the light of the true sun.

They that have their knowledge in this manner are full of spiritual pride and do not see it. They are so blinded with a feigned light that they attribute their self-promotion and lack of toleration to the laws of Holy Church, as if they were submitted in perfect meekness to the gospel and the laws of God. They fancy that pursuit of their own willfulness is freedom of the spirit. Therefore they begin to be like black clouds raining down torrents of errors and even heresies, for the words that they utter in their preaching resound to back-biting, strife, discord, and the pronouncement of judgment on both communities and individuals. Yet they argue that all this is done in charity and a zeal for righteousness. It is not so, for as St. James the apostle says: "Where envying and strife is, there is confusion and every evil work" and "This wisdom descendeth not from above, but is earthly, sensual, devilish," whereas "the wisdom that is from above is first pure, then peaceable, gentle, and easy to be entreated, full of mercy and good fruits, without partiality, and without hypocrisy" (James 3:15-17). Wherever there is envy and contention, there is instability and all sorts of evil work. And therefore the cunning which brings forth such sins does not come from the Father of Light, our God, but it is earthly, beastly, even of the devil.

By these tokens then—pride, presumption, intolerance, indignation, backbiting, and other such sins (for these soon follow after)—the counterfeit light can be distinguished from that which is true. The true sun does not reveal himself in special visitations, granting his light of understanding or perfect love to any soul unless the "firmament" is first made bright and clear of such clouds. That is to say, first the conscience is made pure through

Self-promotion and intolerance are marks of a counterfeit spirituality.

the fire of burning desire toward Jesus, which purges away the mists and impediments of pride, vainglory, ill-temper, envy, and all other sins which beset the soul. As the prophet says: "A fire goeth before him, and burneth up his enemies round about" (Psalm 97:3). This may be taken in the sense of which I speak, that the desire of love shall go before Jesus in the soul and burn away his enemies there, our sins.

Only the meek soul can endure real spiritual light

Unless a soul is first struck down from its height of self-elevation by the fear of God, and is well examined and refined in this fire of desire, purified there from all spiritual filth and dross by long discipline in prayer and other devotional exercises, it will not be able to endure the radiance of real spiritual light nor be able to receive that precious liqueur of the perfect love of Jesus. But when it has been thus refined and made discerning through his fire, then it will be able to bear and receive the gracious light of spiritual perception and the perfection of love—which is the true sun.

So Holy Writ says: "But unto you that fear my name shall the sun of righteousness arise with healing in his wings" (Malachi 4:2). The true Sun of Righteousness, our Lord Jesus, shall rise over you that honor him. That is, where meek souls will humble themselves, considering themselves beneath their fellow Christians, recognizing their own unworthiness and casting themselves down before God, making nothing of their own strengths in *and only in it can the true light shine.* reverent fear and spiritual beholding of him continually, then there will be that favorable climate of perfect meekness in which he shines.

It is unto these souls that the true sun shall arise, illumining their intellects with the knowledge of truth and kindling their affection in flames of love. And then shall they both burn and shine. Through the virtue of this heavenly sun, they shall burn in perfect love and shine in the knowledge of God and spiritual things, for they will then have been reformed in perception and spiritual consciousness.

Accordingly, whoever wishes not to be deceived, I think it might be good for him to avoid prominence and begin by hiding his soul's murkiness from the prying of others, as I have said, trying to forget the pressures of the world altogether so as to follow Jesus in consistent desire, offering himself up in prayer and meditation upon him. For one who does this, the light which follows after the darkness will, I believe, be certain and true, and will shine out of the city of Jerusalem from the true sun. Coming to the soul that travails in darkness while crying out for light, it will show the way and comfort it in its struggle.

I believe that a soul that has truly recognized its own murkiness is not vulnerable to a counterfeit light. That is, when a person truly and unstintingly sets himself to forsake the love of the world, and is enabled by grace to come to spiritual consciousness and self-knowledge, governing himself meekly in that experience, he shall not be deceived by errors, heresies, or fantasies. All of these come in by the gate of pride; so if pride is properly dealt with, these shall not likely find much reception. For the grace which a soul experiences in coming to terms with its own darkness in meekness shall teach it truthfulness and reveal to it thereby which profferings come from the enemy.

IV
LOOKING AT THE SELF

A soul that desires spiritual knowledge needs first to have self-knowledge. For one does not obtain understanding of a kind which is above the self except first there is some self-understanding. And this can only happen when the soul is at peace with itself and appropriately distanced from a preoccupation with worldly things and the senses. It is only then that the soul recognizes itself in its own integrity, undistracted by the body's demands. Accordingly, if you really desire to know and see your soul for what it is, you will not introvert your imagination toward your physical body to discover and experience your soul there, as if it were somehow hidden within your reflective heart in the same way that your heart is hidden and enclosed by your body. If you seek it in this way you shall never find it in itself. The more you seek to discover and experience the soul in the way you would imagine experiencing a physical thing, the further you will be from it. For your soul is not material, but a life unseeable. It is not hidden and enclosed within your body as a smaller thing is hidden and enclosed within something larger; it is, in fact, enclosing and giving life to your body, and is much greater than your body in strength and power.

SPIRITUAL SELF-UNDERSTANDING

So if you want spiritual self-discovery, withdraw your mind from all external physical distractions, even from your five senses as much as you are able, and from remembrance of your own bodily experience as well. Think instead about the rational and spiritual nature of the soul, in the same way you would think about any virtue, such as honesty or humility. [28] In precisely this manner imagine that a soul has a life of its own, deathless and invisible, and has capacity in itself to recognize and know the sovereign truth, and to love the sovereign goodness that is God. When you have grasped this, then you will be beginning to understand something of your own true nature. And look for your self in no other place; for the more fully and clearly you are able to reflect on the nature and worthiness of your rational soul, and come to know it, the better you will see your real self.

Avoid a literal or carnal imagination in spiritual matters.

It is hard going for a soul that is still crude and carnal to have much perspective on itself, let alone to imagine an angel, or God. Right away it falls into the imagination and memory of bodily shapes, naively expecting in this way to obtain self-perspective—as well as a vision of God and spiritual things! Clearly this may not be, since all spiritual things are recognized and known by understanding in the soul, and not by the carnal imagination. Just as a soul "sees" that the virtue of righteousness exists in submission to those qualities which are proper to righteousness, so in the same manner the soul comes to "see" itself by submitting to its own proper means of understanding.

The soul as a mirror

My point is not that your soul should content itself with this kind of self-understanding, but rather that it should by means of this step pursue a higher kind of knowing, above itself, of the nature of God. For your soul is really just a mirror in which you are enabled to see God spiritually. But for this reason you need first to find your "mirror" and then keep it bright and clean from carnal rubbish and worldly vanity, holding it well up from the earth so that

you can see it and our Lord in it. In this life all souls which
are elect are to work to this purpose, in their intention
and desire, even when they are not especially conscious
of doing so.

In this light you will remember my remarking how it is
that many souls in the first stages of their Christian life
have plenty of fervent moments and powerful experiences
of sweet devotion, as they seem to be completely con-
sumed by their first love. And yet they do not have that
perfect love, nor a true spiritual consciousness of God. For
as you well know, though a person feel never so great a
fervor, even when it is so strong that he thinks his body
cannot bear it, and though he be always melting away in
tears, as long as his thinking and his experience of God
are mostly a matter of emotion and not understanding, he
has not yet come to effective contemplation or to perfect
love.

GROWTH IN LOVE

Think of the love of God as having three stages. All are
good, but each successive degree of love is better than the
former.

The first comes only through faith, without there yet
being a grace-filled imagination or spiritual knowledge of
God. This love is in the least soul that is reformed in faith,
and on the lowest plane of charity. And it is good, for it is
sufficient for salvation.

Simple faith

The second stage of love occurs when a soul by faith
and imagination apprehends Jesus in his manhood. This
love, when the imagination is stirred by grace, is better
than the first, since the eye of the spirit is opened in the
beholding of our Lord's human life.

*Imagination of
Jesus in his
humanity*

The third stage of love apprehends, through the manhood of Jesus as it may be seen here, a spiritual apprehension of the Godhead itself. This love a soul will not feel

*A vision of the
Godhead*

until it is reformed in spiritual consciousness.

Souls which are just beginning to come to life and first growth do not have this love, for they cannot yet think on Jesus or love him in a godly way, but rather as it were in a human and natural fashion according to the conditions of his human likeness. Upon that conception of him they shape all their effort, in their thoughts and in their affections. They respect him as a man, and worship him and love him for the most part according to the human imagination, and go no further. For example, if they have done wrong and trespassed against God, they think then that God is angry with them in the same way that a great person would be against whom they had trespassed. Therefore they fall down as it were at the feet of our Lord with sorrow of heart and cry mercy. And when they do this they have a reasonable expectation that our Lord will of his mercy forgive them their trespasses and sin. Now this kind of behavior is very good, but it is not as spiritually mature as it might be.

The limitations of imagination

Such persons, when they worship God, are inclined to present themselves in their thought as if before our Lord's face in a bodily likeness, and to imagine a wonderful light where our Lord Jesus is. Then in this imagination they reverence him, worshiping and honoring him, fully putting themselves in his mercy to do with them according to his will. When they love God consciously they behold him, worship him, and honor him as they would a man, not yet as God in man, but focusing on his Passion or some other event of his earthly life. In this imagination they feel their hearts much stirred up in the love of God.

All this type of worship is good and a channel for grace, but it remains much less and at a lower stage than the effort toward spiritual understanding which occurs when the soul by grace really beholds God in man.

We are called to an apprehension of God himself.

In our Lord Jesus are two natures: his manhood and the Godhead. Just as the Godhead is more sovereign and more worthy than is manhood, even so our spiritual beholding of the Godhead incarnate in Jesus the man is more worthy, more spiritual, and more necessary to us than is the beholding of his manhood alone, whether we conceive of that manhood as mortal or as glorified.

By the same token, the love that a soul feels when considering and reflecting upon the Godhead in human form, when it is revealed by grace, is worthier, higher, and more spiritually valuable than the fervor of devotion a soul experiences in imagination only of his humanity, no matter how much outward emotion that experience produces. After all, the manhood of Jesus is itself already a concession to our humanity. For our Lord does not show himself to the imagination as he is, nor in what he is, for the soul in such a stage of development is not, because of the frailty of our fleshly nature, able to bear it.

A human imagination of Jesus comforts the soul

Nevertheless, this human imagination is given unto souls that cannot yet really think of the Godhead spiritually, in order that they should not err in their devotion, and that they should be comforted and strengthened through some manner of inward beholding of Jesus. They need this to encourage them in fleeing sin and the love of the world. Therefore our Lord Jesus tempers the invisible light of his Godhead, clothing it under the bodily likeness of his manhood, and showing it only to the inner eyes of the soul. Here he feeds us with spiritual love of his precious body. And this love is of such great power that it slays all wicked loves in the soul, strengthening it to endure bodily constraint and distress in times of need, all for the love of Jesus.

but we need to be led on—to love and understanding of his deity.

This experience of love is like a shadowing of our Lord Jesus over a chosen soul. In this overshadowing, the soul is protected from being burned, for just as a shadow is formed by the relationship of light and a body, just so this spiritual shadow is made by the blessed unseeable light of the Godhead and the manhood of Jesus joined to it, as that is revealed to a devout soul. It is of this shadow that the prophet speaks when he says: "Our Lord before our face is a spirit; under his shadow we shall live amidst humanity" (Lamentations 4:20).[29] We are to recognize that our Lord Jesus in his deity is a spirit, and may not be seen by us through the medium of human flesh as he is fully in his blessed light. Therefore we shall live under the "shadow" of his manhood as long as we are here.

Though it is true that this kind of love achieved in the imagination is good, a soul ought nevertheless to desire to have spiritual love, achieved in understanding of the Godhead. It is this height of love which is the final goal and fullness of joy for the soul: all other bodily perceptions are but a means leading us to it. I am not at all saying that we should separate God from the man in Jesus, but that we should love Jesus both as God and as man—God in man and man in God—loving him in a fully spiritual and not a merely fleshly way.

[handwritten marginalia: "shadow" is to protect us from the overwhelming glory of God]

DISCERNING THE OBJECT OF LOVE

Remember Jesus' words to Mary Magdalene.

This is what our Lord was teaching Mary Magdalene, the contemplative one, when he said to her: "Touch me not, for I am not yet ascended to my Father" (John 20:17). We are reminded how Mary Magdalene loved our Lord ardently before the time of his Passion, but her love was perhaps more directed to his physical nature and less to the spiritual. She knew well enough that he was God, but she concentrated little on that fact, for she was not able for it then, and so permitted all her affection and her reflection to be directed toward him as she found him in human form. Nor did our Lord blame her for this at that stage, but praised her greatly.

But afterward, when he was risen from death and had appeared to her, and she would have worshiped him with exactly the same type of love as she had before, then our Lord forbad her, saying, "Touch me not." That is to say, "Do not put your confidence or the love of your heart in that form of man which you see with your fleshly eyes only, to be content with that, for in that form I am not ascended up to my Father. That is, I am not at the same level with the Father, for in the form of man I am less than he is. Touch me not in this way then, but rather set your thought and your love on that form in which I am united with the Father, the form of the Godhead. So love me, know me, and worship me as God, and God in man—not as a godly man after the human fashion. So shall you rightly touch me, for since I am both God and man, and the whole reason I am worthy of love and worship is that I am God and yet took upon myself the nature of man, therefore allow me to be God in your own heart. In your love, worship me with your understanding as Jesus, God in man, sovereign truth, sovereign goodness, and blessed life. For this is what I am." This, then, is what I understand our Lord to have been teaching her, as well as all other souls that are disposed to contemplative understanding and made able for it.[30]

Notwithstanding all that I have been saying, it remains good for other souls who are not yet discerning or made spiritual by grace to keep on directing their love toward God by means of their imagination and human affection, until such time as more grace comes freely to them. It is not sound to leave off any good entirely until we perceive and experience a higher good.

This principle applies also to other experiences which involve bodily feeling: for example, the hearing of delightful music, a sense of warmth and well-being, a perception of light or of sweetness or any physical sensation. These are not in fact spiritual feelings, for truly spiritual feelings are felt in the inner faculties of the soul—principally in love and understanding—and less in the imagination. These other emotions are related to the imagination and are therefore not, in themselves, spiritual experiences. Yet when they are most true and reliable, they are outward tokens of the inward grace which is experienced in the recesses of the soul.

Do not confuse mere emotions with spiritual experience.

The distinction is clearly maintained by Holy Writ in the passage which says that the Holy Spirit appeared to the apostles on the day of Pentecost in the likeness of burning tongues, enflaming their hearts, and "sat upon each of them" (Acts 2:3). Now the Holy Spirit—God himself invisible—truly was not the fire or the tongues that were seen or the burning sensation that was felt bodily. He was invisibly experienced in the depth of their souls, where he lightened their reason and kindled their affection through his blessed presence so clearly and ardently that they had suddenly a spiritual consciousness of truth and the perfection of love. This was even as our Lord had told them, saying of the Spirit of Truth: "He will guide you into all truth" (John 16:13). The fire and the burning were nothing more than a physical manifestation, outwardly witnessing to an experience of grace which was profoundly inward.

And just as it was for the apostles, so it is in other souls that are visited and inwardly lightened by the Holy Spirit, experiencing a similar outward feeling as a comfort and witness to the inward grace. But this type of manifestation is not to be found, I think, in all souls that are being perfected, except where the Lord specifically wills it so. Other imperfect souls can have such an emotional experience outwardly without having received the inward grace. It is not good for them to depend on such feelings too much, but rather to value them only as they help the soul to greater stability of thought in God, and to more charitable love. For some of this kind of experience may be true and some of it feigned, as I have said before.

THE REFORMATION OF EXPERIENCE

Now, I have spoken to you a little already of our reformation in faith, and also touched lightly upon the progress from that initial reformation to the higher reformation that occurs in our experience and spiritual consciousness. I do not at all intend that by these words I should in any way set God's works under a model of my own exposition, as if to say, "This is the way God works in a soul and in no other." No, I mean nothing of the kind. Rather, I am saying according to my own simple sense of it that our Lord Jesus seems to work in this way in some lives. I certainly anticipate that he works otherwise also, in ways which surpass my own understanding and experience.

Nevertheless, whether he works in this or another fashion, by whatever means, over a longer or shorter period, with much or with little effort, if it all comes to one end—that is, to the perfect love of him—then it will be as good to that soul as if the person had been examined, made to endure suffering, mortified, and purified over a period of twenty winters.

Our full "reformation" has but one goal—the perfect love of God.

Accordingly, take what I have said in the spirit in which it is offered, and especially try to grasp my intent. For now, by the grace of our Lord Jesus, I shall try to speak a little of my thoughts on the reformation of our whole manner of perception: what it is, how it occurs, and what kind of spiritual experiences a soul receives in the process.

So that you do not take my speaking concerning the reformation of the soul in spiritual consciousness as some kind of invention or fantasy on my own part, I want to ground it in St. Paul's words, where he says: "Be not conformed to this world, but be ye transformed by the renewing of your mind" (Romans 12:2). That is, you that are by grace reformed in faith do not henceforth conform yourselves to the manners of the world in pride, covetousness, and other sins. Rather, be reformed in newness of spiritual consciousness. Now here you may see that St. Paul speaks of a reformation of experience and consciousness, and what the character of that new consciousness is he develops elsewhere in this way: "For this cause we also . . . do not cease to pray for you, and to desire that ye might be filled with the knowledge of his will in all wisdom and spiritual understanding" (Colossians 1:9). This is what reformation in spiritual consciousness is all about.

You should think of the soul as having two modes of consciousness. The one is external, via our five physical senses. But there is another which is internal, and employs our spiritual senses. These, properly understood, are those special faculties of the soul—memory, intellect, and will.[31] When these faculties are by grace fulfilled in all understanding of the will of God and mature in spiritual wisdom, then the soul will have a new and gracious character of perception. That this is true he shows

This reformation will involve all the faculties of the soul: memory, intellect, and will.

us elsewhere, when he says: "And be renewed in the spirit of your mind; and . . . put on the new man, which after God is created in righteousness and true holiness" (Ephesians 4:23-24). To be renewed in the "spirit of your mind" is not to be transformed merely in bodily feelings or imagination, but in the core of your intellect. When St. Paul says "put on the new man," he means that we should shape ourselves after God in righteousness, holiness, and truth.

Putting off the old man

To explain this further: your reason, which is intended to become the image of God through grace of the Holy Spirit, shall be clothed in a new light of truth, holiness, and righteousness. Then it will be properly reformed in consciousness. For when the soul has a perfect knowing of God, then it is "reformed." So St. Paul says: "Put off the old man with his deeds; and . . . put on the new man, which is renewed in knowledge after the image of him that created him" (Colossians 3:9-10). Suppress in yourself "the old man with all his deeds"—that is, cast off the love of the world and all worldly manners. And "clothe yourself in the new man"—that is, be renewed in the knowing of God after the likeness of him that made you.

Taking on the new

By these same words you understand that St. Paul would have all souls reformed in a perfect knowing of God, for this is the new consciousness that he speaks of everywhere. And therefore, following his words, I want to say something more fully concerning this reformation, as God gives me grace.

Spiritual "milk"

We see that there are two species of consciousness of God. One of these is had principally in the imagination and consists relatively little in real understanding. This kind of knowing is found in chosen souls who are just beginning and growing in grace. These are the souls that love him humanly and not spiritually, with natural affections according to his bodily likeness, as I have explained before. This kind of knowing is good, and it is likened to the milk by which such souls are tenderly nourished as children until they are able to come to the Father's table and receive at his hand whole bread (1 Peter 2:2). Another kind of spiritual consciousness exists, which is principally experienced in the understanding, as it is comforted and illumined by the Holy Spirit; this is relatively obscure at the level of the imagination. For understanding here is the lady, and imagination only her maidservant, serving the understanding as is necessary. It is this higher sort of knowing which is our whole bread, meat for the soul's perfection, and it constitutes a reformation of the whole character of our perception.

The bread and meat of mature understanding

SPIRITUAL INSIGHT

When a soul is called from love of the world, after it is set upright, mortified, and purified, then our Lord Jesus in his merciful goodness reforms it in perception as he sees fit. He opens the inner eyes of the soul when he lightens the reason through a touch of his blessed light, in order that the soul may see him and know him. This does not happen all at once, but little by little at different times as the soul permits him access.

Such a soul sees him not for what he is, for that is not possible for any creature in heaven or on earth. Nor does he see him *as* he is, for that sight comes to us only in the bliss of heaven. But he does see *that* he is, recognizing in him unchangeable being, sovereign power, truthfulness and goodness, blessed life and endless bliss. And the soul sees this, and all that comes with it, not blindly, nakedly, and blandly in the fashion of a student who learns to define him according to his professional instruction and on the strength of mere reason. Rather, the soul sees him in understanding that he really is eternal God, is comforted thereby and lightened by the gift of the Holy Spirit in a wonderful reverence and secret burning love, and with spiritual savor and heavenly delight this soul knows him more clearly and more fully than ever it could be written or said.

Perceiving God is not a matter of mere intellect

This kind of vision, though it be brief and fleeting, is so worthy and powerful that it entirely ravishes the affections of the soul away from the consideration and remembrance of earthly concerns. One's desire is to dwell in such a state forever. And for this kind of perception and knowledge the soul comes to direct all of its affections. Then it reverences God-in-man in his wisdom, marvels over him in his power, and loves him in his goodness.

but a matter of love.

This sight and knowledge of Jesus, with the joyous love that comes of it, may be thought of as the reformation of a soul in faith and spiritual consciousness of which I have been speaking. It is a matter of faith in that it remains cloudy by comparison with that full revelation of him which we shall have in heaven. For then shall we see not only that he is, but as St. John says: "Then shall we see him as he is" (1 John 3:2). And yet it is also a matter of enriched spiritual consciousness by comparison with that blind knowing to which a soul is limited when it first stands in faith alone. For this second kind of soul now knows something of the nature of Jesus as God through his gracious maturity of insight; the first does not yet know it in experience, but merely believes that it is true.

Three stages in the soul's reformation

In order that you may better grasp what I am saying, I shall try to illustrate these three species of the soul's reformation by an example of three persons standing in the light of the sun. Of these three, one is blind, another is able to see but his eyelids are still sealed, and the third has full use of his eyesight.

The blind person has no way of knowing that he is in the sun, but he believes this to be true if a trustworthy person says so. And we can take this person to signify a soul that is only just reformed in faith, and believes in God as the Church teaches, but beyond that knows little. Yet what he has is sufficient for salvation.

The other person sees the light of the sun, but not clearly, either in what it is or as it is, since his sealed eyelids prevent him from seeing more. But he does see the glimmering of a great light. This person can be taken to signify one who is reformed in faith and in spiritual consciousness, and so is contemplative. For he is seeing something of the divinity of Jesus through grace—not fully or clearly, since the lids of his bodily nature form a barrier between him and the character of Jesus our God, screening the person from a clear vision of him. But inasmuch as he sees through this screen by grace, he sees that Jesus is God, sovereign goodness, sovereign being, and that blessed life from whom all other goodness comes.

All this the soul perceives by grace, notwithstanding the impediment of bodily nature. And the more pure and discerning the soul is made, and the more separated from carnality, the sharper is his sight and the stronger his love of the divinity of Jesus. This perception becomes strong enough that even if no other person alive would believe in Jesus or love him, he would never believe or love him the less, for his faith has been reinforced by such true insight and perception that he could not disbelieve it.

The third person, who has full sight of the sun, does not need to believe in it because he actually sees it fully. And this person we may take to signify a blessed soul who without any impediment of physical nature or sin can see openly the face of Jesus in the bliss of heaven. This is no longer a matter of faith, the person having been completely recreated in perception and spiritual consciousness.

There is no condition above the second that a soul may have in this life. The second, however, is an experience of being perfected and brought on the way toward heaven. Not all souls in this state are alike in their experience of vision. Some have it little, have it briefly, and have it seldom; others have it longer, clearer, and more often. Some have by grace an outstanding quality of spiritual vision. Yet all have what we have called the gift of contemplation—of looking toward the Sun of Righteousness.

The soul does not acquire a perfect vision of Jesus all at once. First there comes a little glimmer, after that some growth and development of spiritual consciousness, waxing more mature in the knowledge and love of Jesus as long as life goes on. Truly, I know not what more joy can

Growth in contemplation may be a long process.

be imagined by someone who has enjoyed a little of this growth in vision of him; everything else seems paler and paler by comparison with a clearer sight and love of Jesus, in whom we see all the blessed Trinity.

This kind of vision of Jesus, as I understand it, is like an opening of heaven to the eyes of a pure soul, of which holy men speak in their writings.[32] It is not as some imagine, that the heavens open, as if a soul could see by the faculty of imagination through the skies above the firmament to where our Lord Jesus sits in majesty in a physical light as great as a hundred literal suns. No, it is not like this. Though you could see ever so far out into the firmament in that manner, truly you would not see into the spiritual heaven. And the higher you would ascend above the sun to see Jesus by such imagination, the lower you would actually fall beneath the Sun. Nevertheless, I suppose this kind of imagination is permitted to simple souls who know no better way to seek him who is invisible.

THINGS SEEN AND UNSEEN

What is heaven to a rational soul? Truly nothing else but Jesus, our God. For if heaven is that which is above all other things, then is God alone heaven to man's soul. For he alone is above the nature of the soul. Accordingly, if a soul is enabled through grace to have a knowledge of the blessed nature of Jesus, truly he sees heaven, for he sees God.

Many people err in their understanding of some things spoken of God, not understanding them in a spiritual way. Godly authors indicate that the soul wishing to find God should lift up the inner eyes and seek him above themselves. Then, trying to follow the injunction, some are led to imagine the words "above themselves" in a literal sense, as indicating a higher standing or worthiness of physical place, thinking that one planet in the cosmos is above another in worth or position, and so on. This is not a spiritual understanding. For the soul itself is above all physical creation, not by physical placement, but in the intricacy of its nature. In the same fashion God is above every physical and spiritual creation, not in a physical sense, but in the discernment and worthiness of his unchangeable blessed nature.

Therefore whoever will wisely seek God and find him ought not to run out in his thought as if to climb above the sun and probe the universe, imagining the majesty of God, perhaps, as the light of a hundred suns. Rather, he should in his thought draw down the sun and all the cosmos, as it were, and forget it, casting it beneath even his own small standing place, and setting all creaturely things as insignificant beside the God he seeks. One needs to be thinking in a spiritual manner, both of the self and of God. And if this happens it becomes possible for the soul to "see" above itself, and so "see" heaven.

God cannot be "located" by means of physical or terrestrial knowledge

You should also understand the word *within* in this same way. It is commonly said that a soul ought to see our Lord within all things and within itself. And it is true that our Lord is within all creatures, but not in the way a kernel is hidden within the shell of a nut or in the way that any small physical thing may be contained within one which is greater. Rather, he is within all creatures, maintaining and preserving them in their being by the intricate, ingenious powers of his own blessed invisible nature.

or by probing the physical universe.

Just as something which is most precious and pure is kept in the innermost place of protection, one speaks of the nature of God, most precious, pure, and spiritual, and furthest removed from physical nature, as hidden within all things.

Therefore, whoever will seek God within ought first to forget material things, because of their externality, and to forget also his own body. And he ought to try to forget his preoccupation with his own soul, thinking instead about that uncreated nature which is in Jesus. It is this uncreated nature which has created us, and now enlivens and preserves us, and which gives us our intellect, memory, and will. All of these are inward things, granted through his power and sovereign ingenuity. This is the direction in which the soul should move when grace prompts it to look for the Lord Jesus. Otherwise it avails little to hope to find him within the self and in his creation—at least as far as I can tell.

It is told to us in Scripture that "God is light" (1 John 1:5). This light should not be understood as physical light. God is light in the sense that he is truth and integrity, for truth is spiritual light. Thus it is that whoever most graciously knows truthfulness best "sees" God. The light of truth is likened to physical light for this reason: just as the sun reveals itself to our physical eyes and reveals all other physical things by its light, so the truthfulness of God reveals itself to the rational soul first and then by this light reveals all other spiritual things that are necessary for the soul to know. And so the prophet says: "In thy light shall we see light" (Psalm 36:9). That is—we shall see the truth that is in you by the light which is yourself.

In the same manner it is said that God is a fire: "Our God is a consuming fire" (Hebrews 12:29). This is, of course, not to say that God is the element called fire, which heats a physical body and burns it. Rather, it is another way of saying that God is love, for just as a fire consumes every physical thing that is combustible, just so the love of God burns and consumes all sin and dross from the soul, refining and purifying it, like an intense fire purifying metal.

This sort of language—along with any other figures of speech pertaining to our Lord in the Scripture—is to be understood spiritually; otherwise there is no value in it. There is, however, a good reason for such language being used in Holy Writ to speak of our Lord. We are ourselves so physically oriented that we cannot speak of God or understand his character unless at least initially such language is employed. But when the inner eye is opened by grace to receive a glimpse of Jesus, then shall the soul easily enough refer the metaphors to their appropriate spiritual understanding.

This spiritual opening of the inner eye is what I have

called our reformation in faith and spiritual consciousness. For at this level the soul experiences something in conscious understanding of what it had previously only in naked belief. This extra dimension is the beginning of contemplation, of which St. Paul says: "We look not at the things which are seen, but at the things which are not seen: for the things which are seen are temporal; but the things which are not seen are eternal" (2 Corinthians 4:18). To this kind of vision every soul should desire to come, here in part and then fully in heaven. For in that sight and knowledge of Jesus, the bliss of our rational soul and endless life are fully known. *but we will ultimately leave even them behind, when we see God truly.*

"And this is life eternal, that they may know thee the only true God, and Jesus Christ, whom thou hast sent" (John 17:3).

V

THE GIFT OF LOVE

Now I suppose you are wondering why I speak about this knowing of God as the bliss and ultimate purpose of the soul when earlier on I have said only that one should covet the love of God (mentioning nothing then about this "sight" or perception).

Let me clarify. A vision of Jesus is fullest bliss for a soul not only for the sake of the vision itself, but also for the blessed experience of love that follows from it. Since love comes from knowledge but knowledge does not necessarily follow from love, therefore we say that it is in the knowledge and sight of God principally that the soul has its bliss, and that the more he is known the better will he be loved. But to this knowledge, or to the richer love of God which flows from it, may no one come without a spirit of love. For this reason, then, I have said that you should only covet love.

THE SOURCE OF LOVE

Love is actually the cause of a soul coming to this vision and knowledge—not the love which we have toward God, but the love our Lord has toward sinful souls as yet unable to love him properly. And it is this love which brings us to any knowledge and love of God we may possess, as I shall try to make clear.

Uncreated Love

Godly writers tell us truly that there are two kinds of spiritual love. One is referred to as uncreated, the other created. Love uncreated is God himself, the third person of the Trinity, the Holy Spirit. He is love unformed and unmade. As St. John says of him: "God is love" (1 John 4:8). And we understand by this his Holy Spirit (1 John 4:12-13).

Created love is a spiritual affection instilled in us by the Holy Spirit.

Created love is, by contrast, the affection of the soul inspired by the Holy Spirit, a vision and understanding of Truth—that is, God himself—which is motivated by and focused on him. We speak of this love as created in that it is made by the Holy Spirit. This kind of love is, of course, not God in himself, for it is created; it is the love of the soul which has experienced a vision of Jesus and is directed toward him.

Now you can begin to see why it is that created love is not the reason a soul comes to a spiritual vision of Jesus. For some folks would then be inclined to think that if they loved God ardently enough in their own strength they would make themselves worthy to have a spiritual understanding of him. No, it doesn't happen that way. Rather, it is love uncreated, God himself, who is the cause of all this understanding. For a blind, wretched soul is so far from a clear understanding and blessed consciousness of God's love because of the sin and frailty of human nature that he might never approach it if it were not for the endless bounty of the love of God for us. But because he loves us so much, he gives us the gift of love, his Holy Spirit. He is both the giver and the gift, and makes us by the gift to know and love him.

Now you see the love I was speaking of that you should covet and desire—uncreated love, the Holy Spirit. For truly, no lesser thing or lesser gift than he is himself will suffice to bring us to the blessed sight of Jesus. Accordingly, we ought to desire deeply and to ask Jesus only for this gift of love, that out of the bounty of his love he would touch our hearts with his invisible light so that we might perceive him, and that he would grant to us something of his blessed love so that we might love him as he has loved us.

As St. John says: "We love him because he first loved us" (1 John 4:19). He loved us very much when he made us in his likeness, but he loved us more when he bought us with his precious blood, suffering death for us of his own will in order that we might be saved from the devil's power and the pains of hell. And yet he loves us most intimately when he gives us the gift of the Holy Spirit, who is love, by which we are able to know him and love him, and are comforted, assured that we are his children and chosen unto salvation. On account of this love we are even more indebted to him than we are for our physical creation and for our human life. For though he had made us and purchased us, unless he had also extended himself to us in salvation, what ultimate profit would we have of our created existence or our life? None at all.

The Love we should most covet is the Holy Spirit himself.

Therefore the greatest token of love revealed to us, I think, is that he so offers *himself* in his divine fullness to our souls. He first offered himself in his manhood to his Father in heaven upon the altar of the cross for our ransom. This was a precious gift, and great token of his love. But now, when he gives himself in his divine fullness spiritually to our souls for the effecting of our own personal salvation, enabling us to know him and to love him, then he is loving us without measure, for in this he gives *himself* to us. No more than this could he give. And for this reason it is said that the conversion of a sinful soul through forgiveness of sins is principally the work of the Holy Spirit. For the Holy Spirit is Love, and in the conviction of sin and conversion of a soul our Lord Jesus reveals the fullness of his love, putting away all our sins and taking them on himself. This is the best of all things God may do for a soul, and we experience it personally as a work of the Holy Spirit.

Our created life we associate with God the Father, reflecting on his sovereign might and power displayed in

The Trinity expresses itself toward us in Power, Wisdom, and Love.

creation. Our human life we associate with the Son, reflecting on the sovereign will and wisdom he displayed in his manhood. But the conversion and full redemption of an individual soul by forgiveness of sins we associate with the third person, the Holy Spirit. Herein is the love of Jesus most clearly revealed, and for this he should in turn be most loved by us. For creation is common to us as well as to all creatures, even those without reason. Just as he made us *ex nihilo*, so also did he form the other creatures from nothing; this was a work of great power. And humanity is common to us as well as to all rational souls—Jews, Saracens, and false Christians included. For he died for all souls alike, and redeemed them, if only they are willing to have the benefit of it. And this is sufficient for the salvation of all humanity, even though not all have claimed it; this was, above all, a work of great wisdom. But the conversion and sanctification of our souls by the gift of the Holy Spirit is uniquely a work of love. This is not a common experience, but a special grace granted only to chosen souls. And truly, it is this last which is above all a work of love in us who are his chosen children.

This, then, is the love of God of which I have spoken, urging you to covet and desire it, for this love is God himself, his Holy Spirit. This uncreated love, when it is given to us, works in our soul all goodness, and all that belongs to the good. It is the love wherewith we were loved before we loved him. It convicts us of sin, makes us to love him, and empowers us to withstand sin, stirring us to test ourselves in bodily and spiritual exercises of virtue. This is the love which motivates us to forsake our appetite for the world: it slays in us the wicked promptings of carnal affection and worldly fears; it keeps us from the snares of the devil's temptations; it prompts us to move away from the vanity and excessive business of the world, and from the conversation of worldly lovers. All of this is effected by the uncreated love of God, when he gives himself to us.

For our part, we do nothing at all but permit him to enter in. The most we do is assent to his gracious working in us. And yet even that will is not really our own, but is liberated by him—so much so that it occurs to me to think that everything in us that is well done, whether we recognize it or not, is really done by him. But he does not stop there. Opening the eyes of the soul, he reveals wonderful visions of Jesus, and a knowledge of him which increases as the soul is prepared to receive it. And by such sight of Jesus he ravishes all the soul's affection.

Then does our soul really begin to know him spiritually and to burn ardently in love for him. And then does our soul really see something of the nature of the blessed divine fullness of Jesus—his very deity—and to understand how he both is all and does all things, and that every good deed or good thought comes from him. For he is all sovereign power, truth, and goodness, and therefore every good thing is done in his strength and accomplished by him. And he only deserves the praise and honor for all good deeds, and no one else. For though miserable men try to steal away his honor here for awhile, at the last the truth will be made known that Jesus did it all and men accomplished nothing good of themselves. At that point those who are thieves of the goodness of God, unreconciled to him here in this life, will be condemned to death for their trespass, and Jesus will be fully honored and thanked by all the blessed for his gracious gifts.

The Holy Spirit reveals Jesus in his divine fullness

Of nothing else but Jesus himself, then, is this love which works in our souls, reforming them in spiritual consciousness to his own likeness. This is the love which brings into our souls a fullness of all virtues, making them clean, true, soft, and pliable, and turning them in all respects toward love and affection. (Now the way in which this occurs I shall say more anon.) This is the love which draws the soul away from carnality toward spirituality, from earth-bound experience to a taste of heaven, and from the vain beholding of worldly things to a contemplation of spiritual things and the mysteries of God.

and makes us to be more like him.

THE EXPERIENCE OF LOVE

All this being true, I am led to say that whoever has this love most in his life most pleases God, and shall in turn have the clearest vision of him in the bliss of heaven.

Do not attempt to induce, by your own effort, a sensation of love for God.

As we have seen, this love cannot be had by one's own efforts, as some imagine. It is freely obtained as the gracious gift of Jesus, by those whose hearts have been prepared to receive it. Now some lovers of God apply themselves to loving him almost as if they thought they could induce it by their own effort—straining themselves violently until, breathing heavily, they burst into physical trembling almost as if to draw down God from his heaven unto themselves. So doing they say with their heart and with their mouth, "Oh, Lord, I love thee, and I will love thee. I would for thy love's sake suffer death." And so, in this fashion they experience considerable fervor and grace. Truly, I think, this can be good and rewarding if it is well tempered with meekness and discretion. But for all that, people who look for this kind of experience neither love nor have the gift of love in the manner of which I have been speaking. Nor are they asking for it in the same way.

Simply remain open to him.

A person who has the gift of love through a gracious beholding of Jesus of the sort I mean, or even one that does not have it yet, but desires it, is not feverishly straining beyond his powers, almost as if it were a matter of physical strength to have bodily ecstasies and in that way experience of the love of God. Rather, he merely thinks of himself as nothing and that he can do nothing of himself; he is like something dead in the air, [a seed] borne up and hanging there only by the mercy of God.

Recognizing that it is Jesus who does all and is all, he asks for nothing else but the gift of his love. For since such a person acknowledges that his own love is nothing, he wants the love of God, which is sufficient. And so he prays, and desires that the love of God would touch him with this blessed light, that he might see a little of his gracious presence; then shall he love him. And so by this route comes the gift of love—that is God—into a soul.

The self must decrease if he is to increase.

The more a soul diminishes itself through grace in recognition of the integrity of Jesus without any particular display of outward fervor, and the less it thinks that it has a special love or vision of God, the more nearly it approaches the gift of blessed love. For then it is love which is master, and love which is working in the soul to enable it to forget itself, seeing and beholding the operations of love. In this state the soul is more receptive than active, and such is the condition of pure love. This seems to be what St. Paul is implying when he says: "For as many as are led by the Spirit of God, they are the sons of God" (Romans 8:14). That is, such souls are made so meek and submissive to God that they do not work by their own efforts, but permit themselves to be led by the Holy Spirit, who accords to them the promptings of love which are his own. And these then are especially God's children, and most like unto him.

There are others who cannot seem to love in this way, but who exercise their own affections and stir themselves up through thinking about God and through bodily exercise, trying to draw out of themselves by mastery the feeling of love in ecstasies and other physical signs. They do well and profitably as long as they know meekly that their effort is not producing in itself the gracious consciousness of love, but is in fact a human effort of the soul prompted by reason. And through the goodness of God, because the soul is doing that of which it is capable, these human efforts are converted into spiritual affections, and are redeemed in value as if they had been done spiritually from the start. Here meek souls may see a great courtesy of our Lord, who transforms all our human affections and natural love into the affection and reward of his own love, bringing them all to completion in himself.

These hard-won affections which some folks exercise may be thought of as a kind of belabored spiritual love, as distinct from love naturally engendered by the Holy Spirit. I am not implying that a soul may engender its own human affections only of itself and without grace, for I know well what St. Paul says about our not being able to do any good of ourselves—"Not that we are sufficient of ourselves; but our sufficiency is of God" (2 Corinthians 3:5). For God works in us all, both good will and good work, as St. Paul says elsewhere: "For it is God which worketh in you both to will and to do of his good pleasure" (Philippians 2:13). What I am saying is that such belabored affections are good when made as the efforts of a soul according to the general grace he gives to all his elect. But I distinguish this from special grace made spiritual by a touch of his own gracious presence, as he works in his lovers who, as I have said before, are by him being perfected.

Indwelling Love   In still imperfect lovers of God love works at one remove, mediated by human affections. In perfect lovers of God, love works more nearly by his own spiritual affection. So doing, it displaces in such a soul for a time all other loves, carnal or natural and human though they be. And this is properly the indwelling of Love himself. This love may be had here in part by a pure soul through spiritual vision of Jesus. But in the bliss of heaven it shall be fulfilled by a clear vision of his divine fullness, for then shall no affections remain at all except those which are godly and truly spiritual.

THE PREEMINENCE OF LOVE

Love ought to be sought more than all the gifts   As God for nothing, then, but this gift of love which is his Holy Spirit. For among all the gifts our Lord gives there is none so good, profitable, worthy, or excellent. There is no other gift of God in which he is both giver and gift except this gift of love, and this is the ground of its excellence. The gift of prophecy, the gift of miracle-working, the gift of great understanding and counsel, gifts of great fasting or penitential good deeds: all of these are great gifts of the Holy Spirit. But they are not the Holy Spirit himself. A reprobate and damnable person might have all of these gifts as readily as a chosen soul; therefore, good as they are they are not to be overmuch desired or excessively valued. The true gift of love is the Holy Spirit—God himself—and no one may receive him and remain in damnation, for it is this gift alone which redeems us, making us children of God, heirs to his heavenly heritage. . . .

Covet this love, then, above all things . . . as he bids us in the words of his prophet: "Be still and know that I am God" (Psalm 46:10). You who are reformed in spiritual consciousness and have had your inner eye opened to a vision of spiritual things should leave off for awhile your flurry of visible efforts and take time to "see that I am God." . . .

A soul that has a spiritual vision of Jesus does not make a big issue of striving for virtues. Such a person is not even especially busy about them, but sets all his efforts on preserving his beholding of Jesus. His object will be to hold his mind in stability, binding his love to that alone so that there is no falling away, and forgetting all other impediments as much as possible. And when he is doing this, Jesus truly becomes master in the soul over sin, overshadowing the soul with his blessed presence. Then all other virtues are added naturally. Meanwhile the soul is so comforted and enkindled with the soft feeling of love that it has in its vision of Jesus that it experiences little outward distraction. In this manner Love slays sins generally, reforming the soul in a new experience of virtue.

and more than all the virtues.

LOVE AND MEEKNESS

I want now to say something about how love combats sin and restores virtue in the soul—considering principally pride and its contrary meekness.

You should understand that there are two kinds of meekness. One of them is obtained by the operations of intellect. Another is experienced as a special gift of love. Both relate to love, but in the one case it is mediated intellectually, and in the other it comes directly of love itself. The first is imperfect, the other perfect.

The first kind of meekness is experienced when a person considers his own sins and wretchedness and through

Imperfect meekness is acquired through discipline and intellectual self-appraisal.

this consideration recognizes himself as unworthy of any blessing of God or gift of his grace. Such a person is amazed that God in his great mercy would grant forgiveness of these sins. And because of his own sins such a person is likely to consider himself worse than any sinner alive, and to imagine that everyone else lives better than he does. In the light of this evaluation he thinks of himself as the least of all persons and busies himself to withstand the stirrings of both spiritual pride and pride of appearance as much as possible, indeed despising himself so as not to assent to feelings of pride. If his heart sometimes slips into it, befouled by some vanity of honor, learning, or the praise of others, he is self-critical and repentant as soon as he is aware of his folly, asking God for forgiveness. He discusses the problem openly with his confessor, accuses himself in meekness, and meekly receives his penance. This all constitutes a good meekness. But it is not yet perfect. Rather, it is that sort of meekness which we expect from one who is beginning to grow in grace; it is brought about by a sense of guilt and diligence in dealing with sin. Love produces this meekness in such a person accordingly, through the means of intellectual self-appraisal.

Perfect meekness occurs only in a profound relationship with Jesus

Perfect meekness in a soul is that which experiences a vision of Jesus and a profound spiritual relationship with him. When the Holy Spirit enlightens the intellect with a vision of his true integrity, showing it that Jesus is all and does all, then the soul has such a profound love and joy in the truth of that vision that it entirely forgets itself and fully leans on Jesus with all the love it has, looking upon him. Such a soul is no longer preoccupied with its own unworthiness or its past sins. Rather, it learns to consider the self as not worth considering—with all its sins and all the good deeds it has ever accomplished. It is as if there were nothing now but Jesus.

This is the sort of meekness demonstrated by David when he said: "Lord, make me to know mine end, and the measure of my days what it is; that I may know how frail I am. Behold, thou hast made my days as an handbreadth;

and mine age is as nothing before thee: verily, every man
at his best state is altogether vanity" (Psalm 39:4-5).

Such a person relates to his fellow Christians without
special regard for them or judgment against them as somehow "better" or "worse" than he himself is. For he considers himself and all other persons to be on the same
plane, all in the same way nothing in their own right before God. And this is the truest way of looking at it, for all
the goodness that is accomplished in them or in himself is
only of God, who looks alike upon us all. And therefore
such a person learns to regard other persons in the same
way he has come to regard himself.

and forgetfulness of the self.

This is the kind of meekness reflected in the words of
the prophet Isaiah, when he said: "All nations before him
are as nothing, and vanity" (Isaiah 40:17). That is, compared with the eternal being and unchangeable nature of
God, mankind is as nothing. Out of nothing are we made,
and to nothing we shall return, unless we are preserved in
the being of the One who made us. This is essential truth,
and should make any soul meek that is enabled by grace to
see it.

So when love opens the inner eye of the soul to see this
truth and others that accompany it, then the soul begins
to be truly meek: in the sight of God it sees and is conscious of itself as it actually is. And the soul then leaves
off its self- preoccupation and self-regard, turning fully to
a beholding to him. And when this happens, the soul
considers all the joy and honors of this world as nothing.
The joy of worldly honor becomes such a little thing and
so empty by comparison with that joy and love that it
knows in its spiritual prospect of Jesus, and the knowledge
of his truthfulness, that even if all these other things could
be had without sin, they would be passed up. However
much men would honor him, praise him, favor him, or
offer him high positions, these now would not be a source
of pleasure. And though he had mastery of all the seven
arts,[33] the knowledge of the clergy and of all crafts under
the sun, or had power to work all kinds of miracles, he
would have no more pleasure or fancy in all this than one

might get by gnawing on a dry stick. He would just as soon forget all this and be off alone, out of the sight of the world, as be obliged to preoccupy himself with such things or have the honor of all people.

The heart of a lover of Jesus is enlarged by love

The heart of a true lover of Jesus is so full, grown larger through even a little vision of him and even a little experience of his spiritual love, that all the pleasures and joys of earth are not enough now to fill up even a corner of it. Small wonder it is then that those wretched, worldly lovers who are, as it were, ravished in the love of their own honor and reputation, pursuing after it with all the energy and will they possess, can have no taste of meekness. Indeed, they are amazingly far from it.

But the lover of Jesus has this meekness constantly, and not as a result of arduous effort, but with pleasure and gladness. This gladness, moreover, is not a result of forsaking the world—for that would be the proud "meekness" of a hypocrite—but comes because of a vision and spiritual knowledge of the truthfulness and worthiness of Jesus, obtained as a gift of the Holy Spirit.

and becomes immune to the respect of persons.

That reverent perception and lovely beholding of Jesus comforts the soul so wonderfully and upholds it so powerfully yet tenderly that it it could not be pleased or fully rested in any worldly happiness by comparison; nor could it want it. Such a person simply does not make an issue on his own account whether people blame or praise him, honor or despise him. He neither counts himself well served if men despise him—because it produces more meekness—nor ill served if men honor or praise him—when that is likely to make meekness more difficult. He would rather simply forget both, and only think about Jesus. So he comes in this way to true meekness, for this is much the surer route to meekness.

This is what David was doing when he said: "Mine eyes are ever toward the Lord; for he shall pluck my feet out of the net" (Psalm 25:15). And when anyone does this, he is utterly forsaking himself and casting himself entirely upon Jesus. This is real security, for the shield of truthfulness which he now holds protects him so well that he may not be hurt by any attack of pride as long as he keeps himself behind the shield. As the prophet says: "His truth shall be thy shield and buckler. Thou shalt not be afraid for the terror by night; nor for the arrow that flieth by day; nor for the pestilence that walketh in darkness; nor for destruction that wasteth at noonday" (Psalm 91:4-6). Truth shall equip you with a shield, if you are willing to lay down everything else and look only to him. For then you will not fear the dread of night, the spirit of pride, whether it comes by night or, as he says, as "an arrow that flieth by day."

Pride comes by night to assail a soul in times of despite and the reproach of others, inducing it to fall into heaviness and sorrow. It comes also as an arrow by day when one is being praised and honored by others, whether for worldly or for spiritual action, tempting toward a vain joy or self contentment in this passing glory. This is a sharp arrow, and perilous. It flies swiftly and strikes softly, but its wound is deadly.

> Such love defenc us from the peril of pride.

But the lover of Jesus, who steadfastly beholds him by devout prayer and diligent thinking about him, is so wrapped about with the secure shield of truthfulness that he will not be afraid. This arrow may not then enter his soul, and though it comes it, does not hurt him, but glints off and passes on.

And so, as I understand it, this is how the soul is made meek by the working of the Holy Spirit—that is, by the gift of Love. For he opens the eyes of the soul to see and to love Jesus, and he keeps the soul in that sight restfully and securely; he slays the urgings of pride quietly and softly, so that the soul hardly is aware of it; and he brings in by his truthfulness and loveliness the virtue of meekness.

And Love does all of this, though not exactly in the same measure to all of his lovers. Some have this grace briefly and only in small measure—a kind of beginning, and perhaps a little movement forward in it—because their conscience is not yet fully cleansed by grace. And some have it more fully, because they have a clearer vision of Jesus, and are more conscious of his love. Some have it most fully, for they have the full gift of contemplation. Nevertheless, whoever has even the least of this *quality* of meekness that I have been describing, truly he possess the gift of perfect meekness, because he has the gift of perfect love.[34]

THE QUIET WORK OF LOVE

Love works wisely and gently in a soul where he wills it, powerfully extinguishing short temper, envy, and all passions of anger and self-pity, bringing into the soul in their place the virtues of patience, mildness, peaceability, and warmth toward one's fellow Christians.

Imperfect patience comes of great effort. It is a hard business and demanding of great self-mastery for someone who stands only by the strength of his own reason to maintain patience, holy rest, gentleness of heart, and charity toward his fellow Christians, so that if they trouble him unnecessarily or do him wrong, he restrains himself from any sort of retribution—either in word, or deed, or both—out of the urgings of temper and self-pity. Nevertheless, when such a person is provoked or disturbed in a way which is beyond the strength of his reason, if he is able to restrain his hand and tongue, remaining ready to forgive the trespass when mercy is asked, then we can say that this person has the virtue of patience. This is so even where the virtue is possessed weakly and on its own, as long as the person is committed to having it, works diligently to restrain his irrational passions, and also is sorry when he is not as patient as he would be.

Perfect patience is a gift of love But for a true lover of Jesus to suffer all of this involves no great mastery, because love is doing the fighting for him. With amazing gentleness love extinguishes such urgings of wrath and self-pity, making the soul so easy, peaceable, long-suffering, and godly through a spiritual sight of

Jesus and consciousness of his blessed love, that though such a person be despised and rejected of men, or suffers harm or wrong, shame or villainy, he makes no charges. He is not greatly stirred up against his antagonists. Nor will he let himself become angry with them, for if he were to become roused up he would lose thereby the comfort he feels in his soul. He is the sort of person who may more lightly forget all the wrongs done to him than another person who is able to forgive when mercy is asked. He would almost rather forget it than be required to forgive it, since he considers this the most naturally peaceful response.

And love accomplishes all this, for it is love that opens the eyes of the soul to a vision of Jesus, and stabilizes it **and defends us from the peril of wrath.** with the pleasure of love experienced in that prospect, comforting it so mightily that it is no longer trying to be careful for itself. Whatever men gossip about or do against such a person, it ceases to weigh heavily upon him. And this is because the greatest injury which could be done to him would be something that would interrupt or block his spiritual sight of Jesus. And he would rather suffer all other injuries than to have this happen.

All of this may the soul learn to do well and easily enough, without great troubling of spiritual vision, when the distress is largely an external matter, and does not touch the body—when, for example, it involves backbiting or scorn or the spoiling of possessions. None of this is a cause of real grief. But it cuts somewhat nearer the bone when our flesh is touched and we feel pain; then it is harder. Nonetheless, though it may be extremely hard or even impossible for the frail nature of man to endure bodily sufferings gladly and patiently, without yielding to bitter temper, anger, and self-pity, it is not impossible for love, the Holy Spirit, to accomplish this in the soul he touches with the blessed gift of love. He gives the soul that is in such a plight powerful stirrings of love, and wonderfully fixes it upon Jesus, separating it far from physical awareness through his unique power, comforting it so sweetly by his blessed presence that the soul feels little of the pain and none of the trauma.

Perfect patience under real duress is a grace given to martyrs.

This is a special grace given to holy martyrs. The apostles had it, for as Holy Writ says of them, "They departed from the presence of the council, rejoicing that they were counted worthy to suffer shame for his name" (Acts 5:41). The apostles came rejoicing from the council of the Jews, where they were beaten with scourges, glad that they were counted worthy to suffer any bodily distress for the love of Jesus. They were not stirred up in wrath or animosity to be avenged of the Jews that beat them, in the way a worldly person would be when he had suffered harm, however little, at the hands of his fellow Christians. Nor were they roused up in pride or self-promotion or disdain and judgment of the Jews, as is sometimes the case with hypocrites and people in evident doctrinal error. Such persons will sometimes suffer much physical pain and even death gladly and with a resolute will, as if it were in the name of Jesus and for love of him that they endured torment. Truly this kind of love and gladness in the suffering of bodily mischief is not of the Holy Spirit. It comes not from the fire that burns on the high altar of heaven, but is feigned by the flaming devil of hell. For it is all mixed up with self-promotion, pride, and presumption, and with despite and judgment and disdain of those who punish them. They still imagine that everything they do is charity and that they are suffering everything for the love of God; but they are in fact being beguiled by the Noonday Demon.

It should not be confused with false martyrdom, which is really self-righteousness.

A true lover of Jesus, when he suffers harm from his fellow Christian, is so strengthened in the grace of the Holy Spirit, and made so meek, so patient and peaceable, and all in a truthful way, that whatever wrong or harm he suffers, he always keeps himself in meekness. He neither despises them nor denies them, but prays for them in his heart and has compassion and pity on them, with much more tenderness than even for someone who never did him harm. In fact, he actually loves them better and more fervently desires the salvation of their souls, because he sees that he himself shall obtain spiritual profit on account of them, even though it be against his will. But this kind of love and meekness, above the character of human nature, is accomplished only by the Holy Spirit and in those he makes to be true lovers of Jesus.

Covetousness is also extinguished in the soul by the effects of love, because love makes the soul so covetous of spiritual good that it takes no stock of earthly riches. It has no more delight in possessing a precious jewel than in having a piece of chalk, nor any more affection for a hundred pounds of gold than for a pound of lead. It sets all things that shall perish at one price, and values neither one thing nor another more highly.

Love slays also the sins of covetousness and envy

And it seems good that all these worldly things that worldly men prize so highly and love so fondly should pass away and turn to nought, and with them also the love of them. Therefore a wise person takes thought from time to time of the plight into which these things are afterward to come, and so counts them as nothing. And when worldly lovers strive and fight and plead for earthly goods, the lover of Jesus strives with no man, but keeps himself in peace and considers himself well paid in what he has. This is because he thinks that he needs no more of this world's riches than a scant bodily subsistence; as long as God wills it, he will have that provided for him, and therefore he desires no more. He considers himself well paid in having no more than necessities of the moment, so that he may be freely discharged from the business of security and investment, and fully give his heart and his activity over to the seeking of Jesus, endeavoring in purity of heart to find him. For this becomes the only thing he covets, since only the pure in heart shall see him (Matthew 5:8).

by ordering one's sense of value.

Nor does the ordinary human love of father, mother, and other worldly friends weigh upon such a person. Even that is cut out from his heart with the sword of spiritual love, so that he has no greater affection for father or mother or friend than he has for any other person, unless he sees or experiences in them more grace or more virtue than in other people.

What this comes to is that he would wish that his father and mother had the same fullness of grace as some other folks have; but if they do not, then he loves others better, with a greater charitable love. In this way too, God's love slays covetousness of this world, bringing the soul into a state of poverty of spirit.[35]

Love is doing this work not only in those who have little of this world's goods, but also in some that are in great worldly estate and much opportunity for lavish expenditure. Love extinguishes covetousness in some of these folk, so much so that they care for their worldly prosperity no more than a straw. And if they were suddenly to lose it all, they would not be devastated. This is because the heart of God's lover is, by the gift of the Holy Spirit, so taken up with a vision and love of that which is more precious and worthy that it will not content itself with any contrary affection.

Love also quenches lust But love does not stop here. It extinguishes also the appetite for lechery and all other physical impurity, bringing the soul true chastity in which then it learns to take pleasure. For the soul experiences such delight in its vision of Jesus that it wants to be chaste; and it is no great problem for it to remain in chastity, since there it finds itself most natural and most at rest.

and all excessive appetites. In the same manner the gift of love slays the fleshly lusts of gluttony, making the soul sober and temperate, and bearing it up in such strength that it needs not to take refuge in its appetite for meat and drink. Rather, it takes whatever meat and drink least upsets physical well-being and is conveniently available—not for love of itself, but for love of God.

It comes to this: the lover of God sees well enough that he needs to sustain physical life with meat and drink as long as God permits body and soul to stay together. So this ought to be the sort of discretion that one who has consciousness and experience in love should follow. By whatever means he may most fully keep in grace, and least be prevented from his stewardship through what he takes in bodily sustenance, these are the means the lover of Jesus should choose. Whatever type of meat least hinders and least troubles the heart while it keeps up bodily strength—

be it flesh, fish, or only bread and ale[36]—this is what I believe the soul should choose when it comes to hand.

The whole business of the soul is to think about Jesus in reverent love as much as is possible, without any hindrance. And since there are bound to be some impediments, the less that it is hindered by matters of the table the better. It would be better to eat the best and most expensive food under the sun if that provided less of an impediment to the heart than to eat bread and water when that hinders more. The point is not to obtain some great reward for the pain of fasting, and in the effort be prevented from having a gentle heart. No, the principal aim is to keep one's heart steadfastly fixed on Jesus and in the consciousness of his love. I believe it to be true that one might eat the best of foods of the natural sort with less undue pleasure, and thus do better than another who works all by reason and without love. On the other hand, this should not lead anyone to think he is able to eat the most outlandish fare that by art and artifice is made only for excess; such extravagance we ought not easily to accord with. If little meat (mere bread and ale for example) most helps and eases the heart, keeping it most at peace, then it is better to eat in this fashion.

And yet love does still more. It extinguishes sloth and fleshly idleness, making the soul quick and lively in the service of Jesus. This is so much true that the soul covets always to be occupied in goodness, first of all in an inward beholding of him, by the virtue of which the soul has spiritual delight and a taste for prayer and meditation, and then for all manner of things that need to be done. These things will vary according to the state of responsibility of the person, whether of religious or secular vocation, but all are to be done without grudging or resentment.

Love also reforms idleness

Love also extinguishes vain pleasures of our five physical senses: first the sight of the eyes, so that our soul has no pleasure in any worldly thing for itself, but rather feels pain and distress while beholding it, however fair, precious, and wonderful it may appear. While lovers of the

and quenches inordinate sensuality:

world run out to see novelties of the hour, to wonder at them, and so to feed their heart with vain appearances, a true lover of Jesus is busy to run away and withdraw himself from the sight of such things, so that his inner vision **sight** is not impeded. For he has been seeing spiritually another kind of thing far more fair and wonderful, and he does not want to take his eyes off that for something else.

sound   The same is true for speaking and hearing. It is painful to the soul of a lover to speak or hear anything that might hinder the freedom of his heart from thinking about Jesus. Whatever song or melody or minstrelsy of the outward sort there be, if it prevents the mind from dwelling freely on him in prayer and thought, it gives no pleasure. And the more delectable such things are to others, the more unsavory they are to the lover of Jesus. It is the same with hearing any kind of talk about other persons; unless it touches somewhat upon the exercise of his soul in love for Jesus, it gives no pleasure. In fact, it is very soon irksome. Such a lover would rather be in peace and hear nothing at all and speak no word than to hear the speaking and teaching of the greatest scholar alive, with all the reasoning of human wit at his disposal, unless he could speak feelingly and stirringly of the love of Jesus.

For love is his principal study, and therefore he would not speak, hear, or see anything else except that which could help and further him in a greater knowledge and deeper experience of Jesus. It is beyond doubt that he has no taste for worldly talk; he will tolerate neither worldly tales nor news nor any sort of vain gossip, for none of these pertain to what he loves.

smell, taste, and touch.   And the same is true also for the senses of smell, taste, and touch. The more our thought is distracted and broken off from its spiritual composure by the employment of smell or taste or any of the physical senses, the more we are to flee them. The less we are conscious of them, the better. If we could live in the body without feeling any of these sensations, we would never be distracted by them, yet our senses do often trouble our hearts and put them out of rest. These urgings of the senses cannot, of course, be fully eschewed. Nevertheless, the love of Jesus is some-times so strong in a soul that it overcomes everything that is contrary to it, even these insistent urgings of our bodily senses.

VI
BEHOLDING JESUS

T he human soul, when it has not yet been touched with special grace, is a blunt and rough instrument for spiritual work, able of itself to accomplish almost nothing. Partly this is on account of weakness; of itself it remains cold, dry, undevout, and unsavory. But when the light of grace comes, touches it, and makes it sharp and discerning, then there follows a great freedom and a fullhearted readiness to be submissive to every stirring of grace and to work according to those promptings. And then it sometimes happens that grace moves the soul to prayer. How should the soul then compose itself in prayer?

BEHOLDING HIM IN PRAYER

The most precious prayer that the soul usually employs and the one in which it has most comfort is, I believe, the Lord's Prayer, or else certain psalms from the Psalter. The "Our Father" is particularly apt for illiterate folk, while psalms, hymns, and other prayers of the Church lend themselves to use by people who are more educated.

But when grace is more full in the soul, a person prays any of these in a completely different manner than before, not in the common manner of churchmen, with a loud

In the Spirit, prayer has a different quality.

159

and elocutionary voice, but in a noteworthy stillness of voice and softness of heart. This is because his mind is no longer teased or troubled by outward considerations, but fully at peace with itself, and his soul is set, as it were, in the spiritual presence of Jesus. Therefore every word and syllable is pronounced with heartfelt sincerity, in full accord of lips and heart. The soul is then itself transformed into a fire of love, with each word secretly prayed glowing like sparks flying out from a firebrand, warming all the soul's faculties and turning them toward love. The soul becomes so happily enlivened that the person wishes to pray on and do nothing else. And the more he prays, the better he is able to pray and the more powerful is his prayer. Grace helping ably, all these things become light and easy, so that one turns naturally to psalms and to singing the praises of God with deep spiritual mirth and heavenly delight.

Such spiritual exercise is food for the soul. And such prayer is of great value also in obliterating both secretive and explicit temptations of the devil, even as it destroys the remembrance of worldly pleasures and carnal sins. It bears up body and soul above the painful experiences of our present life; it keeps the soul in a consciousness of grace and the working of love, and it nourishes it steadily just as warmed, fresh wood keeps the kitchen fire going.

It displaces all impediments to communion with Jesus

Prayer like this puts away all irritability and heaviness of heart, helping us to bear them in good humor and spiritual gladness. David models this kind of prayer when he says: "Let my prayer be set forth before thee as incense; and the lifting up of my hands as the evening sacrifice" (Psalm 141:2). That is, "Let my prayer be adorned, Lord, as incense in thy sight. For just as incense cast in the fire makes a sweet smell, its scent rising up in the air, just so a psalm tastefully and softly sung or said in a burning heart yields up its sweet smell before the face of our Lord Jesus and all the court of heaven."

No meat flies dare to rest upon the edge of a pot once it is boiling over the fire.[37] Neither may any carnal appetite light upon the pure soul that is covered and heated in the fire of love, boiling and bubbling up psalms and praises to Jesus. This is true prayer. It is prayer which is always heard by him. It yields in grace to Jesus and it receives grace from him again. It makes a soul feel intimate family warmth with Jesus and all the angels of heaven. Whoever prays in this way will find it a good and grace-filled exercise in itself.

This kind of prayer, though not fully contemplative or by itself the indwelling of love, is nevertheless an important part of contemplation. This is because it cannot be entered into except in a fullness of grace through opening of the spiritual eyes, so that one who has this freedom and gracious feeling in prayer, in spiritual savor and heavenly delight has also to this degree something of the grace of contemplation. Such prayer is a precious offering made in a richness of devotion, received by the angels and presented before the face of Jesus.

The prayer of those preoccupied with the active life tends to have a divided focus, for such folk are often forming in their hearts one set of words which has to do with their business in the world, even as they are sounding in their mouth another set of words—the psalm, for example, being sung or said. Nevertheless, if their intent is true, their prayer will be good and indeed essential, even though it lacks something in savor and sweetness. But the kind of prayer offered by a contemplative person is one of undivided focus. Just as it is formed in the heart, so it sounds in the mouth, as if the thought and pronunciation were one thing. And truly it is not more complicated than that, for such a soul is by grace made whole in itself, so far from fleshly nature that it is master of the body. Then the body becomes nothing else but an instrument, a kind of trumpet of the soul, into which the soul blows sweet notes of spiritual praise to Jesus. I am thinking here of the trumpet that David speaks of when he says: "Blow upon the trumpet in the new moon" (Psalm 81:3). Souls restored to spiritual life through opening of their inner eyes ought to play devoutly, sounding psalms with the trumpet of their tongues.

[margin note:] because it has an undivided focus.

[handwritten margin note:] active life prayer

Since this kind of prayer is so pleasing to Jesus and profitable to the soul, it is good for one newly turned to God, whatever his calling, who wants to please him and obtain a special experience of grace, to desire this kind of prayer experience. In this way a young Christian can be enabled through grace to achieve a liberty of spirit, offering his prayers to Jesus continually in steadfast devotion, and placing his whole mind and burning affection on him. This way he will develop his spiritual instrument for ready use when grace stirs him to use it.

Here is a reliable and faithful kind of prayer experience. If you can achieve it and persevere, you will not be needing to run about here and there asking questions of every spiritual person you meet concerning what you should be doing with your life and how best you can love God, all the while talking about spiritual matters that are well over your head, as some people seem to do. This kind of behavior is not normally very profitable.

Instead, just keep rigorously to your prayers, at first with such labor as is necessary so that afterward you might come to a restful experience of true spiritual prayer. And that will teach you wisdom enough, and honesty without feigning and fantasy. And if you already have this kind of prayer, hold on to it. If grace comes to you by another channel which separates you from it for a time so as to induce spiritual exercise in that manner, then leave it for a time, but always return to it.

Look steadfastly on Jesus. Whoever has this kind of grace in prayer does not need to ask what he shall focus on in his prayer—whether on the formulation of his words, or upon God, or on the name of Jesus—as some people seem to. The experience of grace teaches this plainly enough. In receipt of grace the soul is granted eyes which behold the face of Jesus, and becomes assured that it is Jesus it sees and experiences. I do not mean Jesus as he is in the fullness of his blessed deity, of course, but Jesus as he reveals himself to a purified soul according to the clarity of its vision.

Know this well, that each experience of grace is an experience of Jesus, and according to each measure of grace, more or less, the experience of him is greater or less. Yes, even that first experience of grace in a beginner in faith which we call the grace of compunction and contrition for sin is truly Jesus. It is he who brings about that contrition in a soul by his presence. But at that level of experience, Jesus is known only in simple terms, far from the measure of his divine wisdom, since the soul at that stage cannot obtain a deeper understanding of him on account of its own uncleanness. Afterward, as the soul grows in purity and strength of virtue, it is still the same Jesus who is experienced when the soul is in any way touched by grace. But with greater spiritual maturity comes a more spiritual sense of him, nearer to the divine nature of Jesus.

Truly, the thing that Jesus most desires for any soul is that it be made more godly and spiritual in its vision and in love more like unto him in grace and in harmony with his nature. And this ought to be the goal of all who are his lovers.

You may be assured, then, that any time you feel your soul stirred by grace, especially after the fashion I have indicated, you will in the opening of your spiritual eyes be seeing more and growing more conscious of Jesus. Hold him fast while you may, keep yourself in grace, and let him not depart from you easily. Seek after no other but this same Jesus, and in the experience of his grace you will grow more godly, and grace will grow steadily within you.

Try not to be worried that the Jesus you experience is not Jesus as he is in the fullness of the Godhead, or that you might be deceived by trusting your experience. You may reliably trust, inasmuch as you are a true lover of Jesus, that your experience of him is true and that Jesus is faithfully felt and perceived by you through his grace in the manner in which you are permitted to see him here.

Trust him to reveal himself as he sees fit.

So trust your experience when it is grace-filled and spiritual, and keep it tenderly and in great fondness—not for your own sake but for his sake—that you might be always seeing Jesus and feeling his presence more and more clearly. For grace will always teach you in and of itself, if you allow it to, right to the end of your life.

Perhaps you are beginning to wonder why I say sometimes that grace accomplishes all these things, while other times I say that love works all things, and still other that it is Jesus who does all things, or God. In clarification let me simply say that when I say that it is grace at work, I mean love, Jesus, and God, for all is one and only one. Jesus is love, Jesus is grace, Jesus is God. And because he works all good things in us by his grace for the sake of love, and as God, therefore I use whichever of these terms seems apt as I am moved by the Spirit to write.

JESUS IN HIS WORD

When the soul of his lover experiences Jesus in prayer in the way I have indicated, though that person might imagine that he could never have comparable experience of him by any other means, it sometimes happens that grace puts vocal prayer to silence, stirring the soul to see and experience Jesus in another manner. And chief among these is the beholding of Jesus in his Word. For Jesus, who is all truthfulness, is hidden there, wound in a silken veil of its beautiful words where he may not be known or experienced except with a pure heart.[38] This is simply because truthfulness does not reveal itself to enemies, but only to friends who love and desire it with a meek heart.

To those who approach the Scriptures meekly, Jesus will always reveal himself.

Remember that truthfulness and meekness are true sisters, joined in love and charity. There is no dividing of counsel between them. Meekness is related to honesty; it does not stand alone. Truthfulness—real honesty—always sustains meekness. So they get on together wonderfully well. As much as the soul of a lover is made meek through the inspiration of grace opening his spiritual eyes, it sees that it is nothing in itself, and depends upon the mercy and goodness of Jesus alone, everlastingly borne up by his help and favor. Then it desires only his presence, and so it sees Jesus alone.

In this spirit of approach, we will find the truthfulness

of Holy Writ wonderfully opened up and revealed, far beyond the powers of study and travail and the intellectual reach of our natural human wisdom. And the understanding which we are given there may be thought of as an experience and perception of Jesus.

Jesus is a well of wisdom, and by a little pouring of his wisdom into a cleansed soul, he makes that soul wise enough to understand all of the Scriptures. This does not happen all at once in a special vision, but through that grace the soul acquires a new capacity and a grace-filled talent for understanding it, especially when its words, hidden in our hearts, are called into remembrance.[39]

This opening up and clarifying of our understanding is brought about by the spiritual presence of Jesus. It is just like the gospel says of the two disciples on their way to the castle of Emmaus, burning in their desire and talking about Jesus. Our Lord Jesus appeared to them presently, in the likeness of a pilgrim, and taught them the prophecies concerning himself. And as the Gospel says: "Then opened he their understanding that they might understand the Scriptures" (Luke 24:45). In the same way, the spiritual presence of Jesus still opens the understanding of his lovers who are keen in their desire toward him, bringing to their remembrance by the ministering of angels the words and content of Holy Scripture unsought and unprompted, one after another. And then he readily expounds the Word he sends, however difficult or mysterious.

By his own presence, he will expound their meaning.

The more difficult the Scriptures and the further from the reach of the human intellect, the more delectable is the true revealing of it when Jesus is master. In attention to him it is expounded and declared according to the letter, and in its moral, mystical, and heavenly senses as well.[40] By the letter, which is easiest and most plain, our bodily nature is comforted. In the moral quality of Holy Writ the soul is informed about vices and virtues, and given wisdom by which to distinguish one from the other. In the mystical sense the Word is illumined in such a way

Jesus provides guidance to all levels of scriptural understanding.

that we see the works of God in his holy Church, and learn to apply readily the words of Scripture to Christ our head, and to the Church which is his mystical body. And the fourth sense, called the heavenly, belongs uniquely to the workings of love; this is when all the truth of Holy Writ is applied to love. Because this really is most like a heavenly experience, I call it "heavenly."

These are the intimacies he shares with his friends.

The lover of Jesus is his friend, not because he deserves to be, but because Jesus in his merciful goodness makes him his friend in a true accord. Accordingly, as to a true friend that pleases him in love and does not merely serve him in fear as a slave would do, he reveals his intimate concerns. This is what he was saying to his apostles: "Henceforth I call you not servants, for the servant knoweth not what his lord doeth; but I have called you friends; for all things that I have heard of my Father I have made known unto you" (John 15:15).

To a soul washed clean, which has its spiritual palate so purified from the filth of fleshly love, the Word of God is a lively food and delectable sustenance. It tastes wonderfully sweet when it is chewed upon by spiritual understanding. And this is because the Spirit of Life is hidden there, that quickens all the faculties of the soul and fills them to overflowing with the sweetness of heavenly savor and spiritual delight.

Feeding on the Word

Truly one needs to have white teeth, sharp and clean, to bite into this spiritual bread. Carnal lovers and heretics do not touch the inner pith of it. Their teeth are bloody and befouled; they are therefore prevented from feasting on this bread. By the "teeth" we understand the inner faculties of the soul, which in carnal lovers and heretics are bloody, befouled with sin and worldly vanity. They simply cannot come by the curiosity of their natural understanding to a truthful knowledge of Scripture. Their wit is corrupted by original sin and a life of sin as well, and not yet healed through grace. Therefore they can only gnaw on the outer crust. No matter how much they may talk about Scripture, they experience nothing of its inner good. Not being meek, they are not yet cleansed enough to grasp it. They are not friends of Jesus, and therefore he does not set them at his table and reveal to them his counsel.

The mysteries of God's Word are enclosed under a key sealed with a signet on Jesus' finger—that is, the authority of the Holy Spirit. For this reason, without his love and his life no one may enter in. He alone has the key of knowledge in his keeping, as Holy Writ says, and he is himself the key, and he permits to enter whoever he will through the inspiration of his grace, and does not break the seal.

Jesus does not do this for all his lovers in exactly the same degree. But to those specially inspired to seek after the truth of Holy Writ, with sincere devotion, prayer, and much diligence in study and preparation [he opens up his Word]. And all those who seek him may come to the discovery of him there as our Lord Jesus chooses.

at the invitation of the Lord

See now then how it is that grace opens up our spiritual eyes, clarifying the intelligence so that it is able to rise wonderfully above the frailty of corrupt nature. Grace gives the soul a new capacity to read God's holy Word and to listen to it and think it; it enables the soul to understand truly and richly, and to interpret concepts and words literally spoken in their appropriate spiritual contexts. And this is no great marvel, for the Spirit who expounds and declares his Word in a clean soul, comforting it thereby, is the one who first made it, the Holy Spirit himself. You should understand that this grace may be found just as well in illiterate as in educated persons—at least as pertains to the experience of truthfulness and a taste for things of the Spirit in general—even though illiterate folks do not see all the particulars, which are not in themselves in any case ultimately necessary.

When the soul is thus enabled to have access to Scripture and is enlightened by grace, then it likes to be alone sometimes, away from the constraints of community and its conversation, so as to freely test its intellectual

Making time for the study of Scripture

faculties in probing the truths contained in holy writing. And then come to the mind enough words, good ideas, and concepts to occupy it fully, ordinately, and in sobriety for a long while.

What comfort and spiritual delight a soul may then feel in this good spiritual exercise through its various illuminations: inward perception, intimate knowing, and sudden graces of the Holy Spirit! And the soul may have these by measuring itself against Scripture and in no other way. I believe that one shall not fall into doctrinal error as long as his teeth—his inner faculties—are kept white and clean from spiritual pride or mere curiosity of natural intellect. I believe that David was feeling exuberant delight in this kind of reflection on the Word when he said: "How sweet are thy words unto my taste! yea, sweeter than honey to my mouth" (Psalm 119:103). That is: "Lord Jesus, your holy words indited in Holy Writ and brought to my remembrance through grace are sweeter to my taste, the affection of my soul, than honey is to my mouth." Truly this is a fair and honest work, without painful labor, which lets us see Jesus so richly.

You will recall that there is one kind of vision of Jesus that I have spoken of before, and that is not as he is, but as he is clothed under the likeness of works and words, "in a glass darkly" (1 Corinthians 13:12), in a mirror and by a likeness, as the apostle says.[41]

Jesus is boundless power, wisdom and goodness, righteousness, integrity, holiness, and mercy. And yet we know that what Jesus is in himself in glory no soul may see or hear. Yet by the effect of his working, he may be seen in the light of grace. His power is seen in his making all creation out of nothing; his wisdom is seen in creation's ordinate disposition and his goodness in redeeming his creatures; his mercy is seen in the forgiveness of sins; his holiness in gifts of grace; his righteousness in severe punishing of sin; his integrity in true rewarding of good stewardship. And all this is expressed in the Scriptures, and this is what the soul sees in Holy Writ, along with all other related things.

Know well that gracious understandings of Holy Writ, as well as other writings, are prompted by grace. The Scriptures are nothing else but love letters, epistles between a loving soul and Jesus its beloved, or as I shall say more truly, between Jesus the true lover and the souls loved by him. He has a great tenderness of love toward all his chosen, his adopted children who are still enclosed in the clay of this bodily life. Therefore, though he is absent from them, hid high above in the bosom of the Father and fulfilled in the delights of the blessed Godhead, nevertheless he thinks about them and visits them often through his gracious spiritual presence. He comforts them by his letters of Holy Writ, expelling heaviness and irritation from their hearts, banishing doubts and fears, making them glad and merry in himself. And in his Word he offers true promises to all who are his namesakes and who live meekly in obedience to his will.

The Scriptures are "love letters" from Jesus our beloved.

St. Paul says: "For whatsoever things were written aforetime were written for our learning, that we through patience and comfort of the Scriptures might have hope" (Romans 15:4; cf. 2 Timothy 3:16-17). This is another work of contemplation, to see Jesus in the Scriptures, once our spiritual eyes have been opened. The clearer our sight is in beholding, the more comforted will be our affection in the tasting. Even a little savor of Holy Writ felt in a pure soul should make it set a small price on all the knowledge of the seven liberal arts and other worldly subtlety. For the result of scriptural knowledge is salvation of the soul unto eternal life, while the result of the other is mere vanity and passing fancy, unless it is first converted by grace to serve his higher purpose.

A Still Small Voice

Each of these things I have spoken of—the gift of Spirit-filled prayer and a gracious understanding of Holy Writ—are fair new experiences for a redeemed soul. And if such a soul were to be content with that alone, it might truly be said that it had achieved something of a reformation of experience—though not yet fully. This is because Jesus is always revealing more and leading the soul more deeply into himself, speaking more intimately and in lovelier ways as the soul grows more sensitive to the promptings of his grace.

The prophet Ezekiel wrote: "Whithersoever the spirit was to go, they went; thither was their spirit to go; and the wheels were lifted up over against them: for the spirit of the living creature was in the wheels" (Ezekiel 1:20). Whenever I think of the Spirit moving and the wheels following him, I understand the condition of true lovers of Jesus, well-rounded in virtue without any angularity or frowardness, lightly whirling in the readiness of their will to obey the promptings of grace.[42] For after grace has roused us up and taught us, we are to follow and serve, as the prophets have said.

Recognizing the voice of Jesus within

It is important first to have, however, a certainty of recognition of the voice of grace before we set out, so that we are deceived neither by our own rationalized counterfeits, or by the Noonday Demon. Our Lord said this about his lovers: "My sheep hear my voice, and I know them, and they follow me" (John 10:27). The intimate voice of Jesus is true and reliable, and it leads us into truth. There is no feigning in it, or shades of fantasy, pride, or hypocrisy, but rather gentleness, meekness, peace, love, and charity, and it is full of life and grace. Accordingly, when it sounds within a soul, it is sometimes of such power that a person will suddenly drop everything he is doing—praying, speaking, reading the Word, meditating, or whatever physical work—just to listen carefully. Then, in full attention, hearing and grasping in restedness and love the sweet sound of the Spirit's voice, such a person is utterly ravished from the remembrance of all worldly things.

Sometimes, in such a moment of peace, Jesus reveals himself as an awesome teacher, sometimes as a revered father, sometimes as a lovely spouse. But what we are hearing is his Word, keeping our soul in wonderful reverence and lovely beholding of him, such as is supreme joy to our souls. For we experience such a sense of security and restedness in Jesus, knowing his sustaining favor and goodness, that we would like to live always in this pure moment and not have to do anything else. We feel then as though we are made whole and stable in soul. Reverently we behold Jesus only, as if there were nothing in the universe but him, and knowing that we are held up only by his favor and wonderful goodness.

Often this experience comes without an immediately apparent special insight from the Word, and with but few words formed in our own heart. Yet the effect is of sweet words bringing harmony to our feelings, producing love or worship of him. The soul is readily set apart from the love and pleasure of this world by such a gracious experience, and for the time being even from remembrance of the world. We pay no attention to it because we are preoccupied with listening.

Sometimes there goes along with this experience a whole range of grace-given insights, illuminations which I think of as whispers of Jesus and glimpses of spiritual things. Rest assured that all the work that Jesus does in the soul is to make it a true and perfect bride for himself in the height and fullness of love. Because this work of perfection cannot be accomplished in our slow hearts all at once, Jesus, who is love himself and the wisest of lovers, proves us in diverse areas and by many wonderful means until it all comes about. In order that everything might have the effect of building toward a perfect marriage, he offers such gracious whispers in the manner of one who is courting, wooing his chosen soul to himself.

Jesus' gracious courtship of the soul

He shows us also his jewels, giving us glimpses of the great things he gives, and he promises more, and is winsome in his courtship. He visits often, with much grace and spiritual comfort. Of all the ways he does this I cannot begin to tell you again, and it is not really necessary. But let me say this much, as I am led by grace.

The drawing of a soul toward its fullness in perfect love is known first in the revelation of spiritual things to a soul washed clean, when the spiritual eyes are opened. And this soul does not rest there, but seeks him and loves him who is above every love, without regard for any lesser thing than he is himself. And what are these "spiritual things" of which I speak so often? Spiritual things are simply all that is spoken to us in the truths of Holy Scripture. The soul that is taught to see by the light of grace can see the truthfulness of the Word, and there discern the spiritual things of God.

LORD OF THE UNIVERSE

Among these other spiritual things showed to us in the light of grace is something of the nature of all rational beings and the gracious working of the Lord Jesus in their souls. We might also include the nature of angels, the fate of those blessed and those damned, and a knowledge of the blessed trinity, as grace teaches us.

Holy Scripture says in the Book of the Songs of the Spouse: "I will rise now, and go about the city in the streets, and in the broad ways will I seek him whom my soul loveth" (Song of Solomon 3:20). That is, "I shall rouse up the powers of my thought and go about the city." By the "city" we may understand the universe of all creatures, bodily creation and spiritual, ordained under God by laws of nature, reason, and grace. I go about this "city" when I thoughtfully consider the species and the characters of natural creatures, and also the gifts of grace and bliss of spiritual creatures. In all these I am seeking him whom my soul loves.

Consider the natural and the spiritual universe.

It is wonderful to be looking with the inner eye to see Jesus revealed in creation, to see his might, his wisdom, and his goodness in the ordinance of their various natures; but it is much more wonderful to look upon Jesus revealed in his spiritual creatures. First we can look upon rational souls both chosen and reprobate, to perceive his merciful calling to himself of his chosen. We see how he turns them from sin by the light of his grace; how he helps, teaches, chastises, and comforts them; how he corrects, cleanses, and feeds them; how he makes them to burn in love and light by the fullness of his grace.

We can also consider the reprobate, how rightfully he forsakes them, leaving them in their sinful state, and does them no wrong. We see how he allows them rewards in this world, permitting them to have the fulfilling of their own will, though afterward they are to be punished eternally.

And this is but a little overview of holy Church as it struggles in this life—seeing how black and foul it seems to be in souls that are reprobate, even as it is being fair and lovely in chosen souls. And all this vision is itself a vision of Jesus—not in himself, but in his works of mercy and in his righteous judgments—each day showed and renewed to rational souls. And beyond the pains of the reprobate when we can perceive with our spiritual eyes the joy and bliss of the elect, that is a comfort to us. For his truth cannot be seen by a soul which he has prepared for it without that sight being accompanied by delight and a wonderful gentleness of ardent love.

There is also a perception of the nature of angels, both damned and blessed. The imagination of grace bringing the devil before the eyes of the soul as a clumsy lout bound by the power of Jesus and unable to hurt anyone is edifying and instructive. But then the soul should consider him not in a bodily but in a spiritual way, and regarding his nature and malice, turn him upside down. Scorning and despising him now, it may because of Jesus be unthreatened by that evil. Scripture assures us that: "The wicked are overthrown and are not: but the house of the righteous shall stand" (Proverbs 12:7). In this context the soul may wonder that the devil has so much malice and finally so little power. There is no creature at last so weak, and therefore it is cowardice that makes men so much fear him. He can do nothing without the leave of our Lord Jesus—not so much as enter into a swine, as the Gospel

See how the power of Jesus overturns the threats of the adversary

shows (Luke 8:27-39). Much less, then, may he possess any person who is in the love of Jesus.

If our Lord Jesus does give him leave to trouble us, it is with good reason and in mercy that he does so. And so, welcomed be our Lord Jesus, both himself and all his messengers. The reformed soul no more dreads the blustering of the devil than the rustlings of a mouse. Oh, the devil gets plenty angry with anyone who dares say him nay, but his mouth is choked with his own malice, his hands bound as a thief ready to be condemned and hanged in hell, and so we may in justice accuse and judge him according to his deserts. Do not be amazed by this, for St. Paul meant the same thing when he said: "Know ye not that we shall judge angels?" (1 Corinthians 6:3), angels who are wicked through their malice, though they were made to be good by him. This judgment is an anticipation of his Judgment, and allows contemplative souls to have an inkling of what our Lord Jesus shall do openly at his own appointed time.

The devil will be shamed and disgraced when he fares this way with a soul made clean by our Lord. He would like at last to get away, and cannot, for he is bound by the Holy Spirit, which hurts him more than the fires of hell.

So may we fall before Jesus in meekness and wonder, with hearty praises and thanksgiving that he has so mightily redeemed our simple souls from the malice of so dangerous an enemy, through his great mercy.

JESUS OUR BELOVED

At last then, by this same light, the soul may have a spiritual vision of the splendor of the angels, the worthiness of their nature, their richness of substance,[43] their conformity with grace, and their fullness of eternal bliss. And we may see the diversity of their orders (Psalm 68:17; Hebrews 12:22), and how despite the distinction of persons they all live in the one light of God's eternal truth, burning with love of the Holy Spirit. And we can see how they behold Jesus, loving and praising him in blessed rest without ceasing. And nothing we have ever seen in bodily imagination will have anticipated this because all of our seeing will be spiritual and of spiritual beings.

Then the soul will begin to have close acquaintance with these blessed spirits, and great fellowship. They prove to be most tender and diligent about our souls to help us, directing us, and often through their spiritual presence and a touch of their light driving out phantoms from the soul. And they illumine the soul graciously, comforting us by sweet words suddenly spoken in a heart washed clean by grace. And if any spiritual disease oppresses, they serve and minister to its needs. St. Paul says: "Are they not all ministering spirits, sent forth to minister for them who shall be heirs of salvation?" (Hebrews 1:14).

His angels have charge over us to keep us

These who receive the heritage of health are chosen souls. All spiritual working of words and ideas brought to remembrance, and all similar fair things are part of the ministry of angels when the light of grace shines abundantly in a pure soul. Tongue may not tell the feelings, the enlightening, the graces and special comforts which souls made clean are granted through the ministering fellowship of the blessed angels. And it is such a happy thing to see what they do that the pure soul can scarcely do anything else!

But then, with the help of angels ministering, the soul sees still more. For spiritual knowledge can rise above all this in a pure soul, and that is to a beholding of Jesus—first of his glorified manhood, how it surpasses all the orders of angels, and then of his blessed deity. From knowledge of his creatures we rise to a knowledge of the Creator. And the soul can begin to perceive a little of the mystery of the blessed trinity, and as the light of grace goes before, it will not have error in that knowing as long as it keeps within the light.

and clarify our vision of Jesus.

So it is in this way that the unity in substance and

diversity of persons in the Trinity are made known in its integrity to the eyes of the soul. And many other truths concerning the Trinity will be revealed, such things as are discussed and declared in the writings of reverend theologians of the Church. And believe this, that the very same truths of the blessed Trinity which these godly theologians, inspired by grace, write about in their books for the strengthening of our faith may be known through the light of grace. (I will not say much more about this here; it is not really necessary.)

By gracious understanding we shall come to see him both in his incarnate humanity and as God enthroned.

What a wondrous love indwells the soul, with heavenly delight in the beholding of these truths as they are revealed by special grace. Love and light both go together in a soul washed clean. There is no love born of knowledge and special beholding that may touch our Lord Jesus so closely. For this is the knowledge of Jesus as man and God, the worthiest and highest knowledge there is, because it is of him fully. And therefore it is in this knowing of him that the fire of love burns most brightly of all.

All of these grace-given knowings of the universe of his creatures, and of our Lord Jesus the maker and keeper of all this fair universe, I think of as fair, sweet words of our Lord Jesus to a soul which he will make his true bride. He reveals secrets and proffers rich gifts of his treasure, and arrays the soul withal most attractively. She need not be ashamed in the company of her fellows when she is soon to appear before the face of Jesus her spouse.

All the lovely dalliance of private talk between Jesus and a chosen soul may be called "an hid word," of the which Holy Writ says: "Now a thing was secretly brought to me, and mine ear received a little thereof" (Job 4:12). The inspiration of Jesus is a hidden word, for it is kept secret from all lovers of the world, and kept for his lovers alone. Through this the chosen soul perceives readily the design of his murmurings, which is above all the revelation of his truthfulness. For each recognition of truthfulness, experienced with inward savor and spiritual delight, is an intimate whispering of Jesus in the ear of a soul made clean.

It behooves us, then, to have much cleanliness of soul, in meekness and all other virtues, and to be half-deaf to the jangling and gossip of the world if we really do want to hear these sweet spiritual whisperings of our Lord. This is the voice of Jesus, of which David says: "The voice of the Lord maketh the hinds to calve, and discovereth the forests" (Psalm 29:9). He makes ready the harts, and he shows them the protective woods. It is the inspiration of Jesus which makes our souls as light as deer which leap up from the earth, clearing over all the thorn bushes and briars of worldly vanity. And it is he who shows us the pleasant woods that are his secret hiding places, where the gentle deer may not readily be spied.

Let us then be attentive above all to the voice of the Bridegroom.

The beholding he gives us of himself is truth itself, grounded in grace and in meekness, making our souls wise and burning in desire to come fully before the face of Jesus. And these truths are the spiritual things I have been speaking of, new and gracious experiences of the mercy of God. And in this little book I have merely touched upon these things, for the enhancement of your soul in spiritual wisdom. To be sure, a soul made clean by his grace, and so moved to do these things, may see more of such spiritual things in one hour of grace than could be written in a great book.

"And he gave some, apostles; and some, prophets, and some, evangelists; and some, pastors and teachers; for the perfecting of the saints, for the work of the ministry, for the edifying of the body of Christ: till we all come in the unity of the faith, and of the knowledge of the Son of God, unto a perfect man, unto the measure of the stature of the fullness of Christ."

(Ephesians 4:11-13)

---

[1]Hilton is referring here to a convent or cloister.

[2]The idea of "enclosure" is one drawn from the *hortus conclusus*, or enclosed garden of the Song of Songs, in which the Bridegroom and his spouse have communion. This suggested to men and women of the Middle Ages the value to communion with the Lord of a parallel withdrawal from the "city streets" of the world.

[3]The problem may not have been only the scarcity and high cost of a copy of the Scriptures, but that the woman was not sufficiently versed in Latin yet to read it well. It is clear by the second book (ch. 6), written more than a decade later, that either she had sufficiently mastered Latin or there was perhaps now available to her a copy in English. Modern readers should reflect on the fact that a whole Bible in this period would take a scribe about eighteen months to copy by hand, and that the cost of one copy would therefore be roughly equivalent to the salary of an educated person for that period.

[4]The adverb here has its roots in Hebrews 6:1, Ephesians 4:11-13, and 1 John 4:17.

[5]Hilton puns on "rest"—by which he means both "repose" and "remainder."

[6]Elsewhere, as in his discussion *On Meditation* below, Hilton encourages meditation on the life and Passion of Jesus, as did his contemporaries. But like Wycliffe, he is at pains to distinguish between active contemplation of these things and a naive imagination that picturing the "physical" Jesus is a possible or appropriate aspiration in one's meditation.

[7]Hilton, like all medieval Christians, used the *Ave* (Luke 1:28, 42) and *Magnificat* (Luke 1:46-55) in his daily worship, and would have observed feast days of saints both biblical and medieval (St. Augustine, St. Gregory, etc.) throughout the liturgical year.

[8]In a treatise ascribed to Wycliffe, the scriptural text for the *Ave* prefaces a discussion of Mary's life and character. Wycliffe begins with the familiar words: "Hail Mary, full of grace, the Lord is with thee. Blessed art thou among women, and blessed is the fruit of thy womb, Jesus." He observes that the salutation of the angel Gabriel (Luke 1:28) is here augmented with lines taken from later in the same chapter, the greeting of Elizabeth in verse 42, noting that the names of Mary and Jesus are inserted to make the references clear. He then goes on to say that Mary, in her role as handmaiden to the Lord, is a model not merely for the spiritual life of Christian women but for the humility of every Christian soul in whom Christ would dwell.

[9]See chapter 3, "On Meditation."

[10]Almost no one in the Middle Ages was capable of reading silently. Silent reading was not yet general even in the time of Shakespeare. Similarly, people did not "pray silently" in the way we are accustomed to now. Hilton is referring to a "spirit of prayer" in which one offers his or her thoughts as a kind of continuous prayer.

[11]The phrase in 1 Corinthians 14:14 ("in an unknown tongue") is here understood to refer not to glossalalia but to an "unvoiced" mystical prayer, which is distinct from but not opposed to a more intellectual form of prayer.

[12]Hilton's word is "gracious," which means to him literally "grace-filled." He is referring to meditation on the life of Christ such as might be stimulated by paraphrases of the Gospels, or by painting, stained glass, or the biblical plays so common in his time.

[13]This aspect of spiritual discipline is foundational for Hilton. Without it we cannot know what it really is we are looking for, or what impedes our vision.

[14]The comparison is drawn from St. Augustine's influential book, *On the Trinity*, Books XI and XII. *The Nicene and Post-Nicene Fathers*, ed. P. Schaff (Grand Rapids: Eerdmans, reprinted 1974), vol. 3.

[15]In Hilton's day there were forms of charismatic enthusiasm which sometimes encouraged a devotion to the "Name of Jesus," in which the distinction between the Son of God himself and his name could become blurred. Rhythmic and ecstatic incantation and repetition of the name were, by some writers, suggested as a basic exercise of worship, and even a necessary sign of spiritual vitality. Hilton has obviously heard from the woman to whom he writes that she wonders why he does not ask for the same emphasis.

[16]Hilton is referring to Matthew 1:21, and the correspondence in Latin between *salvum* ("he [shall] save") and *salus* ("health").

[17]Mary the sister of Martha and Mary Magdalene were thought in Hilton's time to be one and the same. See also Introduction, p. xxii.

[18]Hilton's word is "livery"—that is, the special colors and cut of garment that would be distinctive for a nobleman, and would identify his household when they were abroad in the town or surrounding villages.

[19]Hilton suggests that the image of God in us is layered over with our own "image," which is an "image of sin." The sins he specifies, and talks further about in Book II, chapter 5, are of course the Seven Deadly Sins.

[20]The idea of evil as nothingness, or non-being, was developed most fully by St. Augustine. See, for example, his *Confessions* X.43.68.

[21]*Conscience* originally meant something like *consciousness* or *knowledge*, and still bore that weight as *conscientia* in Hilton's reading of St. Paul in the Vulgate Bible. But in his own time *conscience* was becoming more and more identified with the inner witness we speak of today when we talk about our conscience, an identification largely produced by the Pauline passages (cf. Romans 2:15; 9:1; 1 Corinthians 8:7; 2 Corinthians 1:12; 1 Timothy 1:5, etc.). The word can mean either or both things in this text.

[22]As in the *Confessions*, VII.12.18.

[23]Hilton's humor here contains a serious theological point, referenced in part to the verse from Hebrews 11:40 which follows.

[24]This etymology for Jerusalem, *visio pacis*, derives from the connection of Jerusalem with Salem, of which Melchizedek was king (Hebrews 7:1-2), and from early commentaries on the passage.

[25]The popular device of remembrance for those prayers referred to as "common prayer" in Book I, chapter 3, was already in wide general use in the fourteenth century.

[26]Hilton here anticipates John of the Cross in his concept of the soul's dark night.

[27]The "Noonday Demon" was a phrase used to refer to manifestations of satanic temptation which come when a person is in idleness of sloth, not being watchful, "sleeping in the sun" as one commentator has it. In medieval treatises on sin, and even in poems (e.g. *Sir Orfeo*), the analogy is made between this kind of broad daylight appeal of the lie and Satan's approach to Eve in the garden. Hilton's application of the figure to spiritual imposters is unusual.

[28]That is, think conceptually, not as you would about physical entities. Hilton is drawing on the basic distinction, familiar from St. Augustine, between tangible and intelligible matters. The soul is a real entity, but not a physical one. We can conceive of it, but not touch it.

[29]Hilton is clearly only remembering the phrase from Lamentations, perhaps as he heard it in a sermon. His use of these words is not, in fact, properly contextualized in its chapter, but probably is related to medieval commentary on the salutation of Gabriel to the Virgin Mary: "The Holy Ghost shall come upon thee, and the power of the Highest shall overshadow thee . . . " (Luke 1:35).

[30]Cf. note 17 above.

[31]Cf. note 14 above.

[32]Cf. St. Paul, in 2 Corinthians 12 and Acts 7:56. This image is reflected in medieval mystical writers with whom Hilton would likely have been familiar.

[33]The major disciplines studied in medieval universities were seven in number: grammar, rhetoric, logic, arithmetic, geometry, astronomy, and music. Theology was often referred to as the "queen of all the disciplines."

[34]For Hilton it is important to the biblical ideal of perfection as found in Hebrews, Ephesians, and 1 John that one not try to evaluate it quantitatively. The meekness of which he speaks here is to be understood qualitatively, as an attitude of heart.

[35]He seems to be thinking here that some people will "honor their mother and father" out of impure motives, such as, perhaps, the desire to receive a larger inheritance. Behind his statement would seem to lie the words of Jesus: "Blessed are the poor in spirit, for theirs is the kingdom of heaven" (Matthew 5:3).

[36]Bread and ale were common peasant fare.

[37]The reader has here a small reminder of life in an age without refrigeration. Meat would have been brought to the kitchen directly from hanging hooks, in unavoidably fly-infested areas.

[38]The image is Augustinian (On Christian Doctrine), but the point was being made again in Hilton's own time by Wycliffe, who pointed out that discovering Jesus in his Word and not mere words was a matter of purity of intention in the reader's heart beforehand (De veritate sacrae scripturae).

[39]Hilton, like many medieval Christians, and like the Psalmist (Psalm 119:11), believed that it was the word hidden in our heart which was most accessible to the ministry of God's Holy Spirit to our conscience.

[40]The scheme of four levels is common to medieval exegesis, traceable to St. Augustine, and made most widely known in the Middle Ages through the Victorines and other Augustinian commentators. It is found in Dante's Convivio and the prologue to the Wycliffe Bible, where typically the fourth "level" is referred to as "anagogical"—that is, concerned with our progress toward the heavenly Jerusalem. Hilton's emphasis is somewhat unusual, and attractive. The modern Christian may be helped in realizing that really there are only two levels of understanding being talked about, the literal and the spiritual. Hilton's "moral," "mystical," and "heavenly" senses are all aspects of the spiritual understanding of scriptural texts.

[41]The Vulgate text is more helpful to Hilton's exegesis here than the King James. It reads: per speculum in aenigmate ("by a mirror enigmatically").

[42]Cesarius of Heisterbach, a thirteenth-century Cistercian, applied the Ezekiel verse in his Dialogus miraculorum to the spiritual members of Christ's body. Hilton seems to have been aware of a number of Cistercian writers, and may possibly have borrowed this interpretation from them.

[43]Substance, as Hilton and all people of his time used the word, meant exclusively spiritual entity, not what we would think of as "substantial" now at all. The use of the word to mean, as it now almost exclusively does, "material substance," is post-seventeenth century.

Subject Index

"Active" life, 9-10, 34n.1
Analogy and figures of speech, spiritual, 134-39
Angels, 174-76
Anselm, St., xxviii
Augustine, St., xviii, xxviii, 21, 63, 178n.14, 179nn.20, 22, 28, 38, 180n.40
Augustinian rule, xix

Black death, xviii
Body of Christ, 14-15

Canons, Augustinian, xix-xx
Caxton, William, xxixn.4
Cesarius of Heisterbach, 180n.42
Chadwick, Owen, xxx
Christian virtues, 27-29, 43-45
Cloud of Unknowing, xvn.3, xxviii
Colledge, Eric, xxx
Conscience, 61-70, 179n.21
Contemplation of Jesus, 71-83, 122-26, 129-35, 159-77
"Contemplative" life, xxvii, 7-10, 13, 18, 34n.1, 39-40, 42-46
Conversion, 39-40. *See also* Reformation of faith

Dante, 180n.40
David, 75
Doubt, spiritual, 111-13

Exercise, bodily and spiritual, 3-5, 25, 34, 56, 85-86

"Garden of the soul," 82-83
Gardiner, Helen, xxx

Health, spiritual, 66-70
Hilton, Walter
    Coming to Perfection (The Ladder of Perfection), xiii, xiv, xvn.1, xxii, xxiii, xxx, 39-180
    environment, xviii-xix
    Letters to a Layman (Epistle on the Mixed Life), xiii, xiv, xxx, 1-34
    minor works, xxx
    psychology, xxiv-xvii
    writing style, xiii-xiv, xxii
Holy Spirit, xxvi, 52-53, 57, 125-26, 138-39, 146-50, 180n.39
Horstmann, Carl, xiii, xvn.2, xxx
Hughes, Alaphreido, xxixn.3
Hugh of St. Victor, xix

Image of God, xxiii-xxiv, 99-103
    disfigured, 79-83, 100, 179n.19
    restoring, 100-103

Jacob, xxii, 16-18, 34nn.2, 3
Jerusalem, 106, 179n.24
Jesus Christ
    believer's identification with, 59-60

182 Subject Index

as Bridegroom, 177
conqueror of Satan, 173-74
deity of, 123-25
humanity of, 27, 123
imitation of, 78-83, 92-93, 107-8, 146
name of, 68-69, 178nn.15, 16
as revealed in creation, 172-73
seeking and beholding, 73-83, 159-77
John of the Cross, 179n.26
Judas Iscariot, 90-91
Julian of Norwich, xvn.3, xxviii

Kempis, Thomas à, xix, xxii
Kierkegaard, Søren, xxix
Knowles, Dom David, xxixn.6, xxx

Lost Coin, Parable of, xxiii-xxiv, 76-78
Love
 charitable, 8, 78-79, 85-94, 147-57
 "fire of love," 20-21, 48-49, 134
 for God, 107, 121-26, 142-45
 God's, 22-23, 137-41
Luther, Martin, xix

Mary and Martha, xxii, 8-9, 34n.2, 179n.17
Mary Magdalene, 71, 124-25, 179n.17
Meditation, 32-33, 44, 57-60, 178n.6
Meekness, xxv, 45-46, 78-79, 88-92, 107, 116-17, 145-50, 179n.34
Mercy of God, 29, 55-56, 122
Milosch, Joseph, xxx
"Mixed" life, 8-19

Nicholas of Cusa, xxviii
"Noonday Demon," 113-17, 179n.27

Old man, new man, 128-29

Pastoral responsibilities, 10-11, 12, 13
Patience, 150-53
Pepler, Conrad, O. P., xxixn.6, xxx
Pilgrimage, spiritual, 105-10
Prayer, 30-31, 42, 45, 47-56, 159-62
 common prayer, 49-51, 178nn.7, 8, 179n.25
 personal prayer, silent, 54, 178nn.10, 11
 personal prayer, vocal, 51-54

Rachel and Leah, 16-18, 34n.2
"Reformation of faith," xxvii, 121, 130-31
"Reformation of spiritual consciousness," xxvii, 122, 126-29, 131-32
Richard of St. Victor, xix
Rolles, Richard, xxvii
Ruysbroeck, Jan van, xix

Scriptural study, 20, 44, 164-72, 178n.3
Self-examination, xxv, 26-27, 33-34, 61-70, 119-35
Sin
 effects of, 100-102
 love slays effect of, 153-57
 psychology of, 64-66
Sitwell, Gerard, xxx
Spiritual desire, 21-24, 26-30, 41-42, 72-75, 107, 109-10, 111
Stephen, 90

Thurgarton, Priory of, xvii-xviii
Tozer, A. W., xxvi, xxixnn.5, 7, xxvii, xxviii
Truth, xxiv, 88-89

Underhill, Evelyn, xiii, xvn.1, xvii, xxixn.1, xxx

Virgin Mary, 73, 178n.8, 179n.29

Worde, Wynkyn de, xxii, xxixn.4
Wycliffe, John, xvii, xxixn.2, 178nn.6, 8, 38, 180n.40